THE POUND FOR POUND
PRINCIPLE

"Pastor Mike Kai has used what is in his hand, to fulfill what is in his heart. His testimony, good humor, and godly perspective will inspire you to run the race, fight the good fight, and stay faithful to the call of God on your life."

—*Brian Houston, Senior Pastor, Hillsong Church, Sydney, Australia*

"Mike Kai reveals the mind-blowing truth that our strengths and talents are not merely finite, but multipliable and therefore unlimited in reach and potential. His presentation is fascinating and informative, but there's more. *The Pound for Pound Principle* is the kind of book that is such a good read, you forget your world is being changed moment by moment."

—*Miles McPherson, Senior Pastor, Rock Church, San Diego*

"Mike's firsthand testimony of becoming a five-talent guy captures my heart. This book will inspire you to use what God has given you to the fullest. You'll be blessed and will want to share the principles in this book with family and friends."

—*Wayne Cordeiro, Senior Pastor and Founder,*
New Hope Christian Fellowship, Hawai'i

"Mike Kai has a heart for God and God's heart for people. Without exception, whether face-to-face, over the phone, or through an email message, my heart grows larger for God and people as I connect with Mike. I have been challenged by his immense vision for a lost world. I have been humbled by his faith in God's ability to do what seems impossible. I have been inspired by his bold proclamation of the gospel. And I have been encouraged by his hunger for God's Word. If you too hunger for God's Word and are interested in growing your heart, increasing your vision, expanding your faith, and proclaiming the gospel with boldness, read this book. God has gifted Mike with spiritual insight and this insight fills these pages. You will be glad you did!"

—*Don Cousins, Speaker, Author, and Consultant*

"Finally. Hope for us average people. You'll say, 'Wow. Great guy, great stories. I can totally relate.' But beneath the remarkable history of Hope Chapel West O'ahu is a principle Mike won't let us forget. It's not about how special or called we are; the real deal is what we choose to do with what we have. Mike's done a lot, and he will inspire you to do the same."

—*Daniel A. Brown, PhD, Commended to The Word*

"Everyone has a history of experiences in this life; some good, some bad. But not everyone connects the dots. Mike Kai does that and it's what makes him a messenger worth listening to. His message will convert the chaos into clarity."

—*Glenn Burris, President, The Foursquare Church*

"Always the 'underdog,' Mike has learned to multiply his talents and then multiply them again. Happily, his ability to multiply the raw materials of life now results in a large, fast growing church and several church plants emerging from just a handful of people he began to pastor a decade ago. This book will fill you up spiritually. And, it will challenge you to re-assess your use of the 'talents' entrusted to you by our Master."

—*Ralph Moore, Founding Pastor, Hope Chapel Kaneohe Bay, Hawai'i*

"Woven into the story of Mike and Lisa's journey are solid biblical principles, colorful illustrations from the sports world, and self-deprecating humor that make *The Pound for Pound Principle* a combination of spiritual food, life coaching, and commonsense wisdom. All this is wrapped around a story that is a fun read as well as a challenge to make the most of every 'pound' you've been given."

—*Danny Lehmann, Director, Youth With A Mission, Hawai'i*

"The Bible is clear: It's not about how much you've been given, but how much you maximize what you've been given. It's less about portion and more about proportion. Pound for pound, Mike Kai and his energetic Hope Chapel West O'ahu Church have been the living embodiment of God's unique favor for having lived this out. This book will equip and inspire leaders and believers to unleash fresh momentum for a quantum leap to the next level. Get ready to live at a whole new normal."

—*Norman Nakanishi, Senior Pastor, Grace Bible Church Pearlside*

"It seems we live in an age of comparison. We tend to compare ourselves to others in order to either confirm our fears of inferiority or to temporarily squash those tragic fears at another person's expense. What a sad, unnecessary cycle. In his book, *The Pound for Pound Principle*, Mike Kai gives us a path to freedom. He presents with wit, insight, and amazing transparency the principle that the only valid comparison we should ever make is the comparison between what we've been given and what we've done with it. We will all have to give the answer to that question in the future, and Mike's book helps us look forward to that conversation expectantly and with hope. This book just might change your life."

—*Dr. Robert Flores, President, Life Pacific College*

"Mike Kai gives us an important message for all Christians of how we are all gifted, can be used, and will be held accountable. In a wonderful, transparent, personal way, Mike weaves wisdom from biblical principles into an essential fabric of faith. An easy read on some hard facts of life that should give us all hope and a future."

—*Dan Chun, Senior Pastor, First Presbyterian Church of Honolulu*

"The insight and practical wisdom found in Mike Kai's latest book, *The Pound for Pound Principle*, will without a doubt ignite your soul and encourage you to step beyond living a lukewarm, common or mundane life. Mike really helps you unpack your personal potential while empowering you to persevere through obstacles that would hinder you from maximizing your life."

—*Art Sepúlveda, Senior Pastor, Word of Life Christian Center*

"From scrapper to champion, God's odds are always on the runts, the weak and the hungry. Mike Kai is just such a contender and *The Pound for Pound Principle* is his inspiring story of how God takes the 'least likely to succeed' and creates heaven's heroes. Let's DO THIS!"

— *Dawn O'Brien, Hawai'i Media Personality*

"Pastor Mike Kai is one of the most powerful and dynamic Christian leaders in the world today. He never believes that any of the challenges of life are impossible or too hard to overcome. Mike always has an idea that's outside the normal parameters and typical closed box way of approaching ministry. With worldwide relational connections to many of today's most gifted and productive leaders, Mike proves the principles of multiplying the time, abilities and resources that God gives to all of us. This book will motivate you to always believe that God has given us everything we need, to produce more fruit for the Lord of the Harvest. 'Now to Him who is able to do exceedingly abundantly above all that we ask or think, according to the power that works within us' (Ephesians 3:20 NKJV)."

—*Dr. Jerry Stott, South Pacific Foursquare Mission International*

"It is my great joy to endorse Mike Kai. In this life there are path followers and there are trailblazers—Mike is definitely the latter! His magnetic charisma is only surpassed by his impeccable character. Any material generated by Mike Kai will not only inspire you but will equip you as well. In my estimation Mike is definitely in the top 1 percent of leaders in America today. His influence reaches not only locally but also globally. You will be blessed and encouraged by *The Pound for Pound Principle*."

—*Roger Archer, Senior Pastor, Foursquare Church Puyallup*

THE POUND FOR POUND PRINCIPLE

Doing Your Best with What God Has Given You

Michael K. Kai

Authentic

The Pound for Pound Principle
Copyright © 2013
Michael K. Kai

Cover design by Lookout Design

Unless otherwise indicated, Scripture quotations are from the Holy Bible, New International Version®. NIV®. Copyright © 1973, 1978, 1984, 2011 by Biblica, Inc.™ Used by permission of Zondervan. All rights reserved worldwide. www.zondervan.com.

Scripture quotations identified NLT are from the Holy Bible, New Living Translation, copyright © 1996, 2004, 2007 by Tyndale House Foundation. Used by permission of Tyndale House Publishers, Inc., Carol Stream, Illinois 60188. All rights reserved.

Scripture quotations identified ESV are from The Holy Bible, English Standard Version® (ESV®), copyright © 2001 by Crossway, a publishing ministry of Good News Publishers. Used by permission. All rights reserved. ESV Text Edition: 2007

Scripture quotations identified NASB are from the New American Standard Bible®, copyright © 1960, 1962, 1963, 1968, 1971, 1972, 1973, 1975, 1977, 1995 by The Lockman Foundation. Used by permission.

Scripture quotations identified NKJV are from the New King James Version. Copyright © 1982 by Thomas Nelson, Inc. Used by permission. All rights reserved.

Scripture quotations identified The Message are from The Message by Eugene H. Peterson, copyright © 1993, 1994, 1995, 2000, 2001, 2002. Used by permission of NavPress Publishing Group. All rights reserved.

Scripture quotations identified AMP are from the Amplified® Bible, copyright © 1954, 1958, 1962, 1964, 1965, 1987 by The Lockman Foundation. Used by permission.

Scripture quotations identified TLB are from The Living Bible, copyright © 1971. Used by permission of Tyndale House Publishers, Inc., Wheaton, Illinois 60189. All rights reserved.

Italics in Scripture quotations reflect the author's added emphasis. Brackets in all Scripture versions are the author's parenthetical insertions.

Published by Authentic Publishers
188 Front Street, Suite 116-44
Franklin, TN 37064
Authentic Publishers is a division of Authentic Media, Inc

Printed in the United States of America

Library of Congress Cataloguing-in-Publication Data

Kai, Michael K.
    The pound for pound principle : doing your best with what god has given you / Michael K. Kai

ISBN 978-1-78078-100-6
978-1-78078-200-3 (e-book)

To my Lord and Savior, Jesus Christ.
Thank you for all you have done and continue to do in my life.
I would be lost without you. Literally.

To my daughters, Courtney, Rebekah-Taylor, and Charis.
May the Lord bless you in all you do, bringing joy to His heart and a smile to His face. Remember to shoot for the stars and if you miss, you'll hit the moon.

To anyone who has ever felt like an underdog.
May you prevail through your circumstances to be all the Lord called you to be. You are my inspiration.

And lastly . . . to my lovely wife, Lisa.
You are all that I have prayed for and dreamed of.
I am proud to be "Lisa Kai's husband."

ACKNOWLEDGMENTS

First of all, thank you to the people of Hope Chapel West O'ahu. It's been a blessing to partner with you since we first began in 2001. Your love and support for my family and me have been overwhelming.

I would like to thank my mom and dad, John and Esther Kai, for bringing me into the world. You have been incredible parents for Keoni, Lisa, Len, and myself.

I want to thank Pastors Ralph and Ruby Moore, of Hope Chapel Kane'ohe Bay. Thank you for all of the training and encouragement you've given to us over the years. We hope you see our accomplishments and this book as the fruit of your labor. I'm so grateful to Ralph who suggested a year ago, "You should write a book regarding the history of your church," and to John Bevere for encouraging me to just write it.

I would also like to say thank you to the following people who have put in long hours to make this book a reality. Dawn O'Brien, as structure editor, thank you for your expertise, my Big Island sister! Sarah Siu, Koa Siu, Michele Chinen, Joan Tanji, and Melissa Matsuda: thank you for your editing and re-editing. May your sacrifice of sleep and family time be multiplied back to you in spades!

Lastly, the staff at HCWO; I love and honor each one of you for all you do for the Kingdom of God. *The Pound for Pound Principle* is OUR story, isn't it?

CONTENTS

Contents

FOREWORD

The book you now hold in your hands comes from the heart of a man who has done well multiplying what has been given to him. I have had the honor of speaking for Mike Kai on many occasions. He is a dear friend and a strong man of God. His commitment to do his best with what he has been given has resulted in multitudes of changed lives as he pastors one of our nation's most vibrant churches. I believe *The Pound for Pound Principle* has been breathed by the Holy Spirit to empower you as a steward of the gospel of Christ.

Much of this book highlights Mike's personal testimony. He was an "average" boy from small-town Hawai'i—an underdog, by his account—who specialized in entering his dreams through the side door. Whether they arose in the athletic arena, his family life, or his ministerial calling, Mike has never allowed difficulties to deter him from his passions. He does not wait for "fair;" he acts in faith. His story is powerful because it is the gospel. His life proclaims that God has intervened not only to save men, but also to grant them access to greater, more fruitful lives than they could have dreamed.

Many today operate under the assumption that grace automatically eliminates personal effort. We know we are saved by grace through faith, not by our works, but the Bible clearly says we are to "work . . . hard, depending on Christ's mighty power that works within" (Colossians 1:29 NLT). Grace is something upon which we draw to increase the call and gifts given to us. Our participation in the eternal destiny ordained over each of our lives requires perseverance. Mike has discovered what Paul declared to the Corinthian church: God chooses the things that the world calls weak or foolish to confound what it calls strong or wise. As he acts with a spirit of endurance, each Christian can anticipate with joy the "well done" of a faithful servant and receive an entrustment of much in the kingdom of God. This determined stewardship has been the fruit of Mike's own life, and as you read this book, it will—by the holy, empowering grace of God—become the defining characteristic of your story as well. Now sit back and enjoy the powerful words of my dear friend's heaven-inspired message.

—*John Bevere, Author/Speaker, Messenger International*
Colorado Springs / United Kingdom / Australia

INTRODUCTION

Behind every "Cinderella team" is the story of a dedicated coach and players who weren't expected to do much, but they worked and worked with what they had. I cry every time I watch the movie *Rudy*, the true story of an undersized college football player who struggled for years to earn a spot on the Notre Dame Fighting Irish team. I cried in 1983 when Julius Erving, affectionately known as Dr. J for how he operated on the basketball court, finally won the NBA championship title that had eluded him and his teammates for so long.

Today I root for people like decathlete Brian Clay, who continues to defy the odds and the naysayers. Supposedly not tall enough, fast enough, or whatever enough, Brian fought his way through the 2008 U.S. Olympic trials and went on to blow away the competition and win Olympic gold that year. Before Brian hit the world's stage, I was his youth pastor. He is proof that in sports, ministry, and other areas of life, it doesn't matter how "big" or gifted you are. It is your heart and desire, often combined with years of training and sacrifice, that can bring you the type of success you might only dream of.

As you can tell, I have a soft spot for Cinderella stories. From the original Cinderella fairytale of a young woman who goes from years of slumming in rags to success and riches overnight, to real-life Cinderella stories of all kinds, I can't help but to be moved and motivated. It's probably because I see myself as a sort of "Cinder-fella"—an underdog.

The term *underdog* is used often in sports. It originated in the nineteenth century, a time when dogfights were a spectator sport in America and Great Britain. Back then, the winning dog was referred to as the "top dog." The losing dog was typically on the bottom during the match and tagged the "under dog." Today the term is so widespread in the English-speaking world that it is simply one word: underdog.

My penchant for underdog stories has much to do with my upbringing, my physical stature as a youth, and my journey as a one-time single parent. Of course, God had a perfect plan in place. But who would have thought that a twenty-one-year-old divorced father of a two-year-old daughter—someone who once felt abandoned, brokenhearted, frustrated, and suicidal—would ever become a pastor? And who would have guessed he would have been given some of the best training a pastor could ever receive, leave a thriving youth ministry against his will, only to end up loving the adults he would now serve? And who

This book is about doing what you can do with what you've been given, regardless of the amount.

would have considered that this same pastor and his wife would be able to take a church from forty people to more than 3,500 in weekly attendance, plant churches, and speak internationally, all the while bringing the gospel of hope to those who are brokenhearted, abandoned, frustrated, and suicidal?

This book can be described as part autobiography, part history, part principle, part testament, and part Cinder-fella story. Overarching it all is the parable of the talents found in the Gospel of Matthew (25:14–30). There is much to learn from Jesus' story about the three servants who were given different amounts of talents (money). Two of the individuals multiplied their talents, while the other buried his talent. This book is about doing what you can with what you've been given, regardless of the amount.

Sometimes when my wife, Lisa, and I sit in the front row of church, I'll grab her hand and whisper, "Can you believe this, babe? We get to do this for God! Who would've thought?" She'll smile and say, "God is so good." I'll return her nod, close my eyes, and continue to worship Him with the rest of the people in the sanctuary. Of course, I've made my mistakes. Yet God has been gracious and has given me more than I could hope for or imagine. And He is not done expressing His love and blessing upon someone like me and upon you!

My hope is that you will enjoy the story of a Catholic boy from a small town in Hawai'i who somehow became a pastor of a prevailing church. And my prayer is that whether you are a pastor, businessperson, leader, housewife, student, non-profit founder, almost anyone—you'll be inspired to take what you have and use it to your best ability.

Ultimately, one day, our highest hope is to hear the greatest affirmation from the Lord, recorded in Matthew 25:21: "Well done, good and faithful servant! You have been faithful with a few things; I will put you in charge of many things. Come and share your master's happiness!"

THE PARABLE OF THE TALENTS

MATTHEW 25:14-30

For the kingdom of heaven is like a man traveling to a far country, who called his own servants and delivered his goods to them. And to one he gave five talents, to another two, and to another one, to each according to his own ability; and immediately he went on a journey.

Then he who had received the five talents went and traded with them, and made another five talents. And likewise he who had received two gained two more also. But he who had received one went and dug in the ground, and hid his lord's money.

After a long time the lord of those servants came and settled accounts with them. So he who had received five talents came and brought five other talents, saying, "Lord, you delivered to me five talents; look, I have gained five more talents besides them."

His lord said to him, "Well done, good and faithful servant; you were faithful over a few things, I will make you ruler over many things. Enter into the joy of your lord."

He also who had received two talents came and said, "Lord, you delivered to me two talents; look, I have gained two more talents besides them."

His lord said to him, "Well done, good and faithful servant; you have been faithful over a few things, I will make you ruler over many things. Enter into the joy of your lord."

Then he who had received the one talent came and said, "Lord, I knew you to be a hard man, reaping where you have not sown, and gathering where you have not scattered seed. And I was afraid, and went and hid your talent in the ground. Look, there you have what is yours."

But his lord answered and said to him, "You wicked and lazy servant, you knew that I reap where I have not sown, and gather where I have not scattered seed. So you ought to have deposited my money with the bankers, and at my coming I would have received back my own with interest. So take the talent from him, and give it to him who has ten talents.

"For to everyone who has, more will be given, and he will have abundance; but from him who does not have, even what he has will be taken away. And cast the unprofitable servant into the outer darkness. There will be weeping and gnashing of teeth." (Matthew 25:14–30 NKJV)

CHAPTER 1

UNDERDOG

Doing the Best You Can with What You've Been Given

"His master replied, 'Well done, good and faithful servant!
You have been faithful with a few things;
I will put you in charge of many things. Come and share your
master's happiness!'"

Matthew 25:21

My first love was basketball. There's nothing like it, and I still enjoy playing to this day. When I was growing up we lived in rural Hawai'i. The "big city" on our island, Hilo, with a population of 25,000, was an hour's drive away from my hometown, so we often had nothing better to do than play basketball. My dad put up a hoop in the driveway when we were in grade school. If we didn't have baseball or football practice and we finished our homework on time, we'd be in the driveway shooting hoops.

The Kai house was the community center of our neighborhood. Without fail, we would eventually end up playing a game of one-on-one or HORSE, where we would try to outdo one another by making trick shots from all spots on the court. And like siblings often do, fights would break out. We were and still remain very competitive.

When I was younger, it was evident that I was the "little guy," and I developed the complex to go along with it. I viewed myself as an underdog. Today, I stand at an even six feet—though my wife and daughters say I'm stretching it. But in the sixth grade, I was definitely the low man on the totem pole.

My older brother, Keoni, was also a late bloomer and short for his age. In the late '70s, Keoni was away at boarding school in Honolulu and in the seventh or eighth grade. About that time, Randy Newman came out with a lame song called "Short People." I clearly recall Keoni telling my parents how the bigger kids would tease him with that song. When I'd hear it on the radio, I'd turn it off because it would remind me of Keoni and how much I missed him. My own height, that stupid song, my love for my older brother, all of these things contributed to my underdog mentality. And as an underdog, I was in search of heroes—heroes who had been underdogs themselves.

A PARABLE PERSONIFIED

The overriding message throughout my life seems to be summarized in Jesus' parable of the talents found in Matthew 25:14–30. Jesus told the story to his disciples, but I am convinced there are life-changing principles here for all of us.

I presented this parable straight from the Bible earlier in this book, but I want to retell it in my own words to emphasize three things. As you read on, first notice that the master gives *something to everyone*. Second, the servants are expected to multiply the amount they receive. And third, at the end, each is held accountable for what he does or does not do with what he was given.

The parable starts with the master leaving for a long journey. He called his servants to distribute his wealth to them, but he did not hand out the gold talents evenly. He gave it according to their individual abilities. The servant with two bags of gold did what was expected of him and, in time, had four bags of gold! Not to be outdone, the servant with five bags of gold *immediately went to work* and doubled what was given to him, bringing his total to ten bags! When the master returned to settle their accounts, he soon discovered these two servants had passed the test of faithfulness.

The servant who was given just one bag of gold must have felt like the underdog. The problem was, he *did nothing with his portion*. He didn't understand what

I call the pound for pound principle—doing the best you can with you have been given. Much to the master's chagrin, the suspect-servant nervously reported, "I know you are a hard man, harvesting where you have not sown and gathering where you have not scattered seed. I was afraid of your reaction if I failed. So, instead of investing the gold, I decided it was best to bury it under ground, for safe-keeping, of course."

After justifying his poor judgment and lackadaisical attitude, he quickly stuffed his uneasiness. With his chin jutted in the air, the servant cleared his throat and boldly said, "See? I am returning to you what you have entrusted to me. Behold, Master. Please take note and see that I present to you your gold; safe, untarnished and unused, just the way you gave it to me." Then he placed the bag of gold on the table in front of him, patted it lightly, and stepped away.

The master was furious. Calling the servant wicked and lazy, he pointed his finger at him and declared, "You have misjudged me. If that is the way you see me then you should have at the very least put it in a certificate of deposit where it could have earned even some interest. Now, give that one bag of gold to the servant who has ten bags."

The master reined in his anger and sighed. Never one to waste an opportunity for a teachable moment, he told the servants, "Let this serve as a lesson: to those who use well what they have been given, even more shall be entrusted to them. They will have an abundance of my resources. But to those who take my resources for granted, even what little they have been tested with, it will be taken away. Now take this useless servant away and throw him into utter darkness where there will be weeping and gnashing of teeth."

Not surprisingly, the master was filled with joy over the faithfulness of the other two servants who successfully parlayed what he had given them, doubling their investments. "Ah, you have been faithful with a few things," he said, "and have proven yourselves worthy of my trust. Therefore, I will put you in charge of *many things*. Come and share my happiness with me!"

WORKING WITH WHAT YOU'VE GOT

Have you noticed that around the world, especially in developed nations, people place a premium on "bigness"? In almost any endeavor, we want to measure growth or size. In the world of athletics, we size-up athletes by how tall or big they are. Bigger, faster, stronger is what is coveted. Steroids and human growth hormones are illegally administered to athletes looking for an edge.

Christian ministry is not immune to this focus on size. We judge a pastor by how big his church is, how many people attend on weekends. The guy with the largest church is "king of the hill;" everyone else seems to fall behind the one who has "special favor" from God. Now I say all of this with tongue-in-cheek. I'm not a hater of those with larger congregations, as I'll explain in a few paragraphs. Perhaps you have been judged by similar standards—that at first glance your productivity or accomplishments didn't quite measure up to those around you, but what they cannot measure is your potential.

In our case, we started out as a small church of forty people and are now considered a megachurch by those who study church growth. Some even say we are the fastest-growing church in Hawai'i to date. But I'm not impressed, not when there are still over one million people in Hawai'i who are unchurched. Those early days I remember having "church envy" when I'd visit a larger church or hear about a fast-growing one. Maybe it was just me and my underdog/inferiority complex, but it began stirring something in me. I began to wrestle with what I had been given and what I was going to do with it.

> *"But you, Bethlehem Ephrathah, though you are small among the clans of Judah . . ."*
>
> Micah 5:2

As I've mentioned, I was not blessed with great height or stellar athletic ability. In elementary school, I was often picked last for teams by classmates during recess. As if my height and athletic issues were not enough, I was also a sensitive kid—maybe even a mama's boy.

Needless to say, my less-than-impressive combination of height, average athletic prowess, and heightened sensitivity (pun intended) made me fodder for bullies. As such, I eventually developed a vigilante mentality and became a self-seeker of justice and defender of underdogs. Perhaps this is how many super-heroes got their start, though this is not necessarily a category I place myself in. But I digress.

Back then, little came easy for me. Hardly the smartest kid in the class, I was closer to the middle, the best-of-the-mediocre. I had to work hard for A's and B's and remember struggling for a C+ in geometry.

It was even difficult to excel in the sport I love, basketball. I was cut from the ninth-grade junior varsity team and cut again two years later from the varsity squad. After each cut, though, I worked hard and made the team the following year.

To my surprise, the major highlight in my high school athletic career came on the football field. In my senior year, at five-foot-nine and just 130 pounds, I tried out for football for the first time and became a starting wide receiver. I was even named to the all-conference honorable mention team. At my size, I had to learn to be crafty without the ball and definitely fast after it was thrown to me! Whether in practice or in a game, when I caught a ball I would run with my eyes as big as silver dollars and as fast as my legs would take me for fear of getting the lights knocked out of me. To this day, I still hound my mom, teasing her, "If you had kept me back for a year I would've dominated and had a college scholarship and possibly made you rich! But no, you had to rush me into preschool just because I was a December baby."

In almost every case, when it came to basketball, baseball, or football, if things did not turn out right for me the first time, I would not give up. I would bounce back, practice hard, and return the following year to make the team. This process would repeat itself over and over again in my young life.

Who Said Life was Unfair

In the parable of the talents, the master owned everything and *gave* the three individuals all they possessed. That principle is simple to grasp: God owns it all—our gifts, abilities, money, relationships, church—everything. It's also important to understand that the master provided the servants with no instruction. He abruptly left for an undisclosed amount of time and then surprised the servants with his sudden return. Thankfully, you and I have been given the greatest book of all to instruct us, the Bible. But the part that really resonates with me is this: What the servants had is all they had. Today we constantly hear athletes on TV and elsewhere overuse the phrase "It is what it is" to describe a situation that is, well, the way it is. And in Jesus' parable, it was what it was. The servants had no say in what they received, and what they did with what they had was their choice.

Jesus explained that before the master left on his journey, he distributed the talents (or abilities, which we will use as a reference) to each servant as he saw fit. The master undoubtedly knew what he was doing, proving his judgment correct in the end. But again, it is interesting to note that he gave each servant a designated amount of talent according "to his own ability." This tells me the

❧

What I have been given is all up to me.

❧

master knew how much each person could handle. To the first, he gave five talents. To the second, two talents, and to the third, one talent. In our society, some might say, "Wait a minute. That's unfair! Shouldn't each person be given an equal amount of talents? Each should get 2.67 talents!" I understand that. And wouldn't it be great if every sixteen-year-old basketball player was six-feet tall? Then we could say, "Let the best man win!" Of course, in life all is not "fair," at least at first glance.

I see two lessons in this parable: Everything comes from God, and what I do with what I have been given is all up to me. This stirs several reactions in me, perhaps for you too. For starters, I am motivated to see how much I can do with what I have been given, whether it's a little or a lot. Another side of me wonders why I did not get as much as the guy with five talents. I want to complain: "Lord, why wasn't I bigger in school, smarter in class, better looking than some of the other guys? My childhood and adolescent years would have been so much easier." Still another part of me scoffs at the guy who buried his single talent. I cannot help but think, *There is no way I'm letting the master return and discover I let the two other dudes beat me!*

Now that I am older and having to prove myself on an athletic field or in a classroom is behind me, I realize I have been a two-talent guy all my life. Five-talent guys, at least to some, are Microsoft's Bill Gates, evangelist Billy Graham, or pastors of megachurches. Five-talent women are adventurer Amelia Earhart, Foursquare Church founder Aimee Semple McPherson, or golf prodigy Michelle Wie. It's so easy to think, *Oh, I could never be like them*, and that's the problem. What tends to happen is that we begin diminishing what we have when we measure it in the light of someone else's lamp.

It's good to remember that five-talent people almost always work hard to earn their five-talent status. They can also sacrifice much and suffer heartache and pain. While a missionary in China, Sister Aimee, while pregnant with their first child, lost her husband of less than a year. Throughout Michelle Wie's childhood and teenage years, she had to put in many long hours at the driving range. Then there's the remarkable journey of NBA star Jeremy Lin. What makes his story so inspiring is that he is thriving after being cut from two teams, laboring in a developmental league, and basically sitting on the last spot on the bench until the Knicks had no more healthy players or answers to a long losing streak. He became an "overnight sensation" with the Knicks and has since joined the Houston Rockets.

Although these individuals had to work to fulfill their God-given potential, from birth they were each "graced to do what they were called to do,"[1] as my friend and author John Bevere describes. In other words, their destinies were already assigned to them, yet they still had to work very hard. But through grace, God enabled them to be tenacious, dedicated, and committed to become who they were destined to be.

For me, I have learned that I have been called and blessed to do what I now do. Today, some assume I am a five-talent guy (FTG) because of the size of our church. That's not for me to decide. But I'm pretty sure I started off as a two-talent guy who had five-talent potential. Some might say that my wife, Lisa, and I pastor a five-talent church (FTC). At this point, I would say that they're right. But, trust me, we sure did not start that way.

I am convinced that the perceived FTGs and FTCs of this world are not necessarily born, *they are made*. And they have what they have because, over time, they have proven themselves worthy of receiving what they have been given.

How? Through dedication, hard work, and a tenacious spirit that translates into rewards, that's how.

So, how do we become five-talent people? That's the question I used to ask. However, I believe each of us should instead ask, "Am I doing everything I can with what I've been given? Am I maximizing the one, two, or five talents the Lord

What matters most is that you are using what God has given you to the best of your ability.

has blessed me with? In what areas of my life can I prove myself faithful so that I can receive all He has planned for me, thereby bringing much glory to him?"

In light of the parable of the talents, it's not whether you have been given one talent, two talents, or even five talents. What matters most is that you are using what God has given you to the best of your ability.

Did I complain about being shorter than some of the kids in my class when I was younger? Sure I did. When we started the church, did I ever ask God why I hadn't received as many "talents" as others? Sure, more than once. But there had to be a point when I stopped looking over the fence (or the basketball hoop) and focusing on what others had. I needed to quit whining about what I didn't have and start thanking God for what he had already entrusted to me.

Each of us needs to wake up and work on what is and will be, rather than lamenting about what wasn't. We need to ask ourselves this critical question: What am I doing with what I've been given?

THE WEIGH-IN IS THE WAY UP

I'm not a huge boxing fan, but I consider myself a fan of good boxing. During my high school years in the 1980s, the matches for supremacy in the boxing world seemed to involve three fighters: Marvin Hagler, Thomas Hearns, and "Sugar" Ray Leonard.

"Marvelous" Marvin Hagler, the bald-headed, goatee-sporting fighter with a menacing look and a right cross hook to equal his appearance, dominated the welterweight division. At the same time, out of Detroit, Michigan, came a tall and lanky southpaw (left-handed) boxer named Thomas "Hitman" Hearns (don't you love the nicknames?). His long reach prevented many a fighter from getting too close to him. Hearns faced Hagler in 1985. What a fight! In the end, Hagler got the better of Hearns.

That epic fight set the stage for the rise of wildly popular, pretty-faced "Sugar" Ray Leonard, one of the sweetest and smoothest boxers of all time. Sugar Ray, the quickest boxer of the era but by no means the strongest, would taunt his opponents with a mesmerizing windmill with his right, then follow up with a quick left-jab that seemed to stun his opponent from the trance. He would then do a quick shuffle-step dance that wowed the crowd and stick his head out as if to say, "Go ahead, I dare you to hit me." The fans would go crazy whenever Sugar Ray, with his Michael Jackson-like Jheri curl hairdo, had momentum on his side. What a showman! I remember the pandemonium of watching a Leonard–Hagler bout in 1986 on satellite screens at the Honolulu Blaisdell Center and Leonard coming back in the 12th round from what seemed to be a Hagler sure-win.

It was a glorious time for boxing, even to the average teen like myself. I had seen a little bit of Muhammad Ali and heard of his "Thrilla in Manila" fight. I had witnessed the ferocity and ear-biting techniques of Mike Tyson. But no boxers captured my imagination like the Hearns–Hagler–Leonard trio. Though the glory seemed to be in the heavyweight division with Ali's generation of boxers and in the 1990s with fighters like "Iron" Mike Tyson, Evander Holyfield, and the renewed George Foreman, none could duplicate the excitement that the smaller guys of the 1980s seemed to generate. The latter seemed to be quicker on their feet, hungrier, and more determined, scrapping for everything they could get whether the stakes were victory, glory, or respect. It was exciting to take in!

Boxers, no matter their weight class, are judged by their wins versus losses. It gets interesting when we try to determine the all-time best fighters, especially if they compete in different weight classes and never fight each other. Experts and everyday fans argue a fighter's pound-for-pound (P4P) value. They take into account how many championship belts a fighter earns. They look at his knock-outs, his weight class, his opponents' records, and so on. These sorts of evaluations take place in almost all sports (including mixed martial arts), but none more than in boxing.

You might be thinking, Okay, Mike, where are you headed with the boxing illustrations? Let me start with this: The size of a fighter isn't as important as the effectiveness of a fighter.

Today, pound-for-pound, many consider the Filipino Emmanuel "Manny" Pacquiao to be the best of the best when it comes to boxing. Some argue that Pacquiao, nicknamed Pacman, is the best P4P fighter in the history of the sport. I'm not a boxing expert, but at the least, Manny, who is a little over five-feet six inches and 150 pounds max, is certainly worthy to be called this generation's best P4P fighter. His record at this time is 54 wins, 2 losses, and 4 draws. And to add to his legend, 38 of those wins have been by technical knockout (TKO).

Let that sink in for a moment and consider again that he's the size of the average Filipino male. His biceps are 13 inches, chest (expanded) is 41 inches, and his reach is 67 inches. If you saw Manny walking down the street and did not recognize him, you would never know he is one of the greatest boxers of all-time with a devastating right hook. However, it's what you don't know from first impressions that can be most impressive.

The average size of a boxer in the heavyweight division begins at two hundred pounds. Pretty impressive. But if you read enough about Manny Pacquiao, you'll see a different "stat" mentioned over and over. What people admire but can't measure in Manny Pacquiao, or any fighter for that matter, is the size of his heart.

Of course, we aren't talking about the actual size of the organ that pumps blood to a boxer's fists of stone. Nor does his heart have anything to do with good intentions. When Pacquiao steps through the ropes and the "tale of the tape" is put aside, he and his opponent stand in the center of the ring, staring into each other's eyes for any sign of fear, daring the other to blink. The only thing measured when the bell rings and the referee yells "Box!" is the size of the heart of the boxer—his dedication, his hard work, his tenacity.

Not all boxers are created equal. Some are taller than others. Some are a little more talented, muscular, quicker, or whatever. Some are naturally gifted and seem born to knock the living daylights out of another man. Some grew up defending themselves against street punks who tried to extort their lunch money. Some found the only way out of the inner city was to punch their way out of it.

Whatever the talent level or motivation for boxing, what it all boils down to is summarized in this statement I've heard since I was a kid: *"It's not the size of the dog in the fight that matters, but the size of the fight in the dog."* Now before you call PETA on me, wouldn't you say that statement holds a lot of truth in it?

Now, take what we've just been talking about and apply it to almost anything. Here's what I believe: One of the great measurements of a church, a leader—and you and I and everyone else—is our P4P value.

What you do with what you've got—the size of your heart—that's the pound for pound principle.

---

[1] John Bevere, *Extraordinary: The Life You're Meant to Live* (Colorado: WaterBrook Press, 2009), 130.

CHAPTER 2

CONTENTMENT

Finding It in Your Pound for Pound Value

"And the Lord said, 'Who then is the faithful and wise manager,
whom his master will set over his household . . . ?'"
Luke 12:42 ESV

"Do you see a man skilled in his work? He will stand
before kings; He will not stand before obscure men."
Proverbs 22:29 NASB

Jesus said, "To whom much is given much is required." He also said, "If you're faithful with a little, I'll put you in charge of many." These two verses naturally lead to this question: What are you doing with what you've been given? Notice I haven't made a case for bigger is better. I haven't said success is everything.

What I do want you to take to heart is that we are called to bear fruit (John 15:5). And when I refer to fruit, I mean tangible evidence and results in our lives to our being faithful to what the Master has given to us. I am also making a case that you and I have a responsibility to use what we've been given no matter the size of our church, our education or training (or lack of it), or whether we think we're not this, that, or the other thing. Again, what it boils down to is this: What are you and I doing with what we've been given?

What Is the P4P Church?

The P4P church is a church that is doing the best it can with what it's been given. I sometimes come across pastors who feel bad because their churches haven't grown larger than hoped for. They've either plateaued or can't seem to close the "back door" or both. Some started off with more than they

> ### We have a part to play that is more than just great Bible teaching.

currently have. Some have served for years and have never gone above a certain number in attendance and have felt like a feeder church to the larger churches.

I remember feeling that way in the early days. Before we moved into our new building (a story I'll share later), I remember struggling for the first five years to somehow generate enough momentum to keep us growing every year. You might know the maxim, "Feed the sheep and God will build the church." That's a really great saying, but I think it's incomplete.

We have a part to play that is more than just great Bible teaching. I remember the struggle to be viewed as somehow legitimate, in my mind and our church's mind. There were churches much bigger than ours with heftier budgets, more engaging programs, and nicer facilities, and . . . air conditioning! For our first eight years we met in a school cafeteria that seated 225 people maximum with an open beam ceiling. It would get so hot in our Hawaiian summers (from April to October) that it was like having church in a sauna or Crock-Pot. In fact, I probably only wore a sweater once a year in that old cafeteria because it rarely dipped below seventy degrees inside. When it did, there was much rejoicing!

I used to ask myself, *How can we compete?* But that was the wrong question. For one, I saw those other churches as our competition rather than our complement. In my heart, I secretly viewed other churches from a position of envy rather than rejoicing with them. Thankfully, I came to realize the devil is our competition. But worst of all, there was a time I set my eyes on what was yet to be harvested rather than what was already in the barn. I needed to get back to stewarding who and what had been given to me. I needed to get back to "seeking and saving that which was lost." Why would the Lord of the Harvest entrust me with more if I haven't been faithful with what I've already been given?

When it comes to the P4P value of a church or ministry, I can empathize with pastors who struggle. When I think about the discouragement that may be affecting their psyche, I think about the pastor who's been faithfully serving his congregation for five, ten, twenty years and hasn't seen his church grow further than he hoped. He's heard the church-growth gurus who say if you don't pass a certain benchmark within the first two years, the chances of ever passing that mark will simply fade each subsequent year. He feels defeated when he attends conferences or denominational gatherings because he's reminded of what he doesn't have. He begins questioning whether he has the "right stuff" to be a "successful" pastor. He starts to doubt his calling as other churches seemingly zoom by.

It's not that anyone is intentionally putting him down for a lack of numerical growth. It is just that he desires to grow and becomes frustrated when it is slow in coming. When he begins to compare himself to the guy with "five talents," all of the labor he has invested over the years begins to diminish in his eyes. Comparison is a dangerous activity.

If you are in a similar situation to what I've just described, please do not lose heart. I am convinced that if you've been a faithful steward of the talent or talents God has given you, you'll hear the words one day, "Well done, my good and faithful servant. Enter into the joy of the Lord!" I do not believe God will greet you, or anyone for that matter, with a statement of reprimand just because you had a smaller congregation than a pastor of a large church.

Imagine if you heard the Lord say, "Welcome, Jim! It's good to see you. Ahem. Let me see. According to our records, you appeared to struggle to get your church past your next benchmark set for you by church growth experts. To be quite honest, we are very disappointed. I know you weren't given as much as some of the mega-church pastors, but we expected you to do at least half what they did. And, of course, we know we didn't call you to a major metropolis with millions of people but that doesn't matter because, you see, I'm an unjust master . . ." I don't believe for a moment this will happen in heaven. On the contrary, there will be rewards handed out for faithfulness.

I think of the pastor in a small town or village who's faithfully serving as a bi-vocational pastor. He has a full-time job at the local factory and he's a full-time pastor. His wife works outside the home and their children attend the public school down the street. They struggle to make ends meet. The church can't sustain a full-time salary for their pastor, let alone twenty hours per week, so they pay him a monthly stipend. This may cover his mobile phone bill and provide for a modest resource budget that allows him to attend a few local area conferences per year. There's just enough money to rent the building on weekends and fund some outreach. If he wants to attend a conference in another state or another country the church will have to save up for an entire year. Yet, it is arguable that he has less time to prepare sermons, minister to his flock, and even operates on less sleep than most people. He loves what he's been called to do but it is all taking a toll on him emotionally and physically. Yet he remains faithful to the congregation he loves and equally faithful to the Lord's calling. In the final tale of the tape, his faithfulness is really all that matters.

By the Numbers

I'm a numbers guy, I must admit. I like pie charts and graphs better than plain documents and spreadsheets because you can visualize trends. Seeing numbers this way allows you to quickly compare data over weeks, months, even years. At our church we count every child, teenager, and adult who makes a decision to surrender to the Lord. That number is precious to me, so we make sure we get it right.

We count attendance, tithes, and offerings. Service after service we count. We count because we are accountable. In fact, Jesus counted when He explained how the shepherd left the ninety-nine sheep to go after the one who wandered off from the flock. The shepherd would have meticulously taken roll in order to know one had gone AWOL. Counting is important.

We celebrate church attendance and growth. It is worth commemorating! Whenever we hit a new benchmark we always pause and throw a party. It is a privilege to pastor the flock, and with thankfulness and prayer we devour cake and ice cream and don't forget the balloons. Then we move on as if to say, *Thank you, Lord. What's next?* When you're growing, everything is great! This is when you love numbers and you love counting. But if growth plateaus, or worse, numbers decline, it can be quite frustrating. Hopefully, though, it causes the leader to become motivated. Motivation and inspiration go hand in hand. In fact, *I believe inspiration is the fuel of motivation.* Being inspired gives one a motive for achieving.

Everybody needs inspiration and motivation. I think of a child who will shoot for straight A's on her report card because she'll receive a reward from her grandmother. Someone in sales will go the extra mile if inspired by an award trip somewhere special.

Reviewing the numbers every weekend helps me to know how we are doing. I don't believe there's anything wrong with that. It's like the dashboard on my car. It tells me key things such as how fast I'm going and how much gas is left in the tank. The gauges on the dashboard indicate if my engine is overheating or not. They also tell me if my oil is running low. Dashboard gauges are critical to driving a vehicle. I believe counting is equally important to leading a church.

When our "gauges" showed numbers had leveled off or were declining, the frustration I sometimes felt was an extra motivation to pray. I was more open to new ideas. After all, if doing the same things over and over again wasn't getting the desired results, something had to change! That can be a good kind of frustration or, may I coin the phrase, *a sanctified frustration?* Like inspiration, frustration can often be the catalyst to motivation.

Having a type of dissatisfaction with things while tempering your heart is a good thing. I've had a saying for several years now that has been reshaped over time: *"I'm always content but never complacent."* Please hear my heart on this. What I mean is that I am grateful for what the Lord has blessed us with. There is no doubt about that. We would not be where we are today if it were not for His hand on our lives. As Psalm 16:5 (NASB) says, "The Lord is the portion of my inheritance and my cup; You support my lot." No matter what, I can rest in my contentment, His blessings, and in who I am in Christ.

Yet one might be tempted to think: *I do feel content, so shouldn't I just take it as a sign to kick back, relax, and let God do all the work?* Of course, if this type of thinking were true, we should all close our doors and resign from our positions, become monks in a desert monastery, and be content with everything around us while the rest of the world literally goes to hell.

No, godly contentment is a gift; as Paul wrote, it is considered great gain (1 Timothy 6:6). Yet we must not allow ourselves to become complacent and think, *This is good enough, don't you think? Let's just enjoy this for a while, pat ourselves on the back for a job well done. We've already exceeded our own expectations, so why work harder?*

Somebody, please say something, shoot me, anything (not really), if you ever see or hear of me pulling back and becoming complacent. I want to do more, become more, and reach for more. I believe God wants to bless you and me with more. But becoming *more* and reaching *more* isn't all about you or me. It's about impacting the lives of others. In fact, it's bigger than that; much bigger. It also includes the lives beyond those you directly impact. Just think who could be changed if we press on, remain faithful, and prevail.

The Trap of Complacency

Contentment is being thankful for what I currently have. Certainly I would love to have "more." And, I intend on getting better and becoming more, but I am not going to make the mistake of overreaching.

To overreach would be like an out of shape, forty-five-year old who thinks he can play basketball for the Chicago Bulls, and in his driveway holds his own press conference and announces that he's looking for an agent so he can turn pro and enter the NBA draft! That'll be one sad and lonely guy waiting for his phone to ring while eating chips and salsa on his overstuffed couch with an overstuffed ego. That's some serious overreaching!

On the other hand, as we strive to avoid overreaching, we can easily allow complacency to settle in. Complacency can lead to underachievement. Guard yourself from it. Avoid it. Sometimes I feel like I have this sanctified frustration knowing that we can do and become more for the Lord. I get frustrated when

I feel as though we are not reaching or living up to our potential. Don't get me wrong. I'm not walking around the house kicking my dog or walking in the church and yelling at the receptionist.

Yet, no matter how big our church is, I'm content but never complacent. Why content? Because Jesus is my Lord, I'm saved, my wife and children love and respect me, and we pastor an awesome church. I am very thankful and therefore content, *but the moment I allow myself the perceived luxury to cruise into complacency will be the moment the church joins me there as well.* As I've heard pastor Bill Hybels say, "Speed of the leader, speed of the team."[1]

I'm content but never complacent.

Complacency puts you to sleep and leads you into mediocrity. It gives us the picture of someone who is uninvolved or disengaged. Or worse yet, it describes someone who has abdicated his or her leadership. Complacency keeps us from doing our best and reaching our God-given potential. It stifles creativity and excellence. It could possibly stem from an attitude of arrogance or pride. It starts the moment you say to yourself, *I've arrived.* Or, it could mask itself in your stubbornness to stick to the way you've always done things even if they aren't working. This stubbornness causes a person to dig in his heels as if to say, "If it was good enough for my daddy, then it's good enough for me!" Do you see it?

I try to avoid complacency in my health, my marriage, my family, and our church. Again, please don't misunderstand me. I am not a super-driven, win-at-all costs Gordon Gecko type of person. I adhere to the Sabbath, take my vacations, and have even been on a two-month sabbatical. But if I become complacent, I will fall behind. To me, it would be like burying the talents the Lord has given me.

I think a question to ask ourselves frequently is, "Have I been faithful to steward well what God has entrusted to me?" Hopefully there are many seasons for all of us when it is easy to be motivated and inspired to diligently serve others. Discipline can be leveraged and used to multiply our talents and abilities to the glory of God. On the flip side, there are bound to be times when we are naturally less than enthusiastic about the work ahead. We might be tempted to go through the motions—to do something without our heart fully engaged to the task. Whatever we do, we must not become complacent.

You and I have been entrusted with time, relationships, people, and money. There is an expectation placed upon us to steward them well. Take what you have been given and do the best with what you have. Don't allow things like fear, discouragement, laziness, and indecision ("analysis paralysis") to stop you. It is unacceptable to the Master and should be to you as well.

USE IT OR LOSE IT

When it comes to the P4P principle, if we do nothing with what is given to us, we risk losing it! In the more than eleven years of Hope Chapel West O'ahu, I'm sure I have "lost" people because they felt they were not shepherded well. They might not have articulated it to us as such, but we have had our share of people leave. I'm not talking about the ones who are church shopping.

Complacency will cause even a "five-talent" person to bury what they have.

Sometimes you have no control over that because for one reason or another, people are trying to find the right fit for them and their families. That's not a problem to me. The sooner they discover whether they are called to our church, the better it is for everyone.

However, if we fail to steward, shepherd, or lead those entrusted to our care, then we've got to ask ourselves, "What can we do that is *within our control* to ensure it doesn't happen again?" If there are things to change, we need to do it. If *we as leaders* have to change, then adjustments should be made. In fact, not changing when change is required is very similar to burying the talent.

Complacency will cause even a "five-talent" person to bury what they have. We become less prone to take risks (even calculated risks for that matter) and operate

19

with less faith than in the past. We become fearful of losing what we have. We kick into self-preservation mode to protect what little we think we have left. Generosity drops with time, talent, and resources. Our influence diminishes.

If things get to this point, you may hear yourself (or people around you) repeat phrases such as "We can't afford to do that" or "With a church of our size, we have to really be careful. . . ." If someone hears me utter these sorts of things, I hope they ask, "What happened to the guy who took risks in spite of his fears? Why did you change, Mike?"

I am not a reckless renegade. I understand the concept of making wise, prayerful decisions. This is sound advice for those who are younger, as well as older. But who said that we would have to slow down when we got older? Is that how apostle Paul operated? I don't think so. He went as hard as he could as long as his body and mind allowed him to. In fact, I think the only thing that truly slowed him down was a Roman cell and eventual death.

You don't have to be older to have this type of slowdown. It can even happen while we're young. Previous failed attempts or temporary setbacks can cause us to become overly cautious to a fault. When we are more concerned about personal preferences or styles and aren't flexible to make course corrections in key moments, we are in danger of losing the talent. If we shrink back from seeking big dreams and visions because we fear we can't achieve them, we may very well lose what we currently have. It will then go to a wise and faithful steward. It's as simple as that. I've seen it happen. And it's as if the Lord was saying to me, "Okay, Mike. I'm giving you a chance. Steward them well, son."

It's in Your Head

I've been blessed with three beautiful daughters, but I've always said that if I were to have a son, I would name him Caleb. Why Caleb? For one, the Old Testament's Caleb didn't receive as much attention as Joshua. But that's understandable, even though Caleb was the other spy with Joshua who displayed great faith (Numbers 13). But what I love about Caleb is his *different spirit* as recorded in Numbers 14:24.

When he finally arrived in the Promised Land as an old man, Caleb said (and I paraphrase Joshua 14:10–12): "I was with you when we saw the land and when we were stopped by the cry-babies who were afraid and wanted their mommies. And I've been with you for the last forty years. And you know what? I'm still young despite my age. In fact, I can still do what the younger kids can do and the difference is I've got experience to back up my muscle. I can still take 'em! So, give me my land! I'll take the hill country. I'll drive 'em out and they'll be sorry they ever set eyes on this old warrior. Give me my land!"

I want to have the same spirit as Caleb when I am his age (in forty years or so). I want to be able to take new ground even when others are retiring. If the Lord lets me live that long, I want to keep doubling the talents He's entrusted to me and sharing them with those who have also been faithful. That is what I hope to do. What you do with what you've been given makes all the difference.

---

[1] Bill Hybels, *AXIOM: Powerful Leadership Proverbs*, 2008 (Grand Rapids, MI: Zondervan, 2008). https://www.amazon.com/Axiom-Powerful-Leadership-Bill-Hybels/ dp/031027236X

CHAPTER 3

"WHO'S IN MY CORNER?"

Trusting in Key People to Get You Going

"Though one may be overpowered, two can defend themselves.
A cord of three strands is not quickly broken."
Ecclesiastes 4:12

Every great fighter needs a great team in his corner. No matter how good a fighter is, he will never reach top billing as a prizefighter without the help and support of those who are in his corner. Prizefighters are not born, they are made. And behind every prizefighter is a story of his relationship with those in his corner.

In all my life, never did I imagine I would become a pastor. In fact, growing up I never met a pastor, nor could I tell you what a pastor was. When I went to my high school guidance counselor's office to take a vocational test, the profession "pastor" wasn't even listed. I'm pretty sure it is still not listed. Raised as a Roman Catholic I was an altar boy for seven years and received the Sacrament of Holy Confirmation at Our Lady of Lourdes Catholic Church. Still, the thought of becoming a pastor was far removed from me.

FAMILY

I grew up in Honoka'a, a plantation town of 2,000 people on the Big Island of Hawai'i. I could not have been raised in a more beautiful setting. The Big Island is home to several microclimates. Imagine in a span from sun up to sun down being able to drive to the summit of Mauna Kea (elevation 13,796 feet) where it snows from December to February, then driving back down to walk on ancient lava flows as arid as a desert, then driving for an hour to explore a tropical rainforest, all in one day. Although I have been to several countries since becoming a pastor, the Big Island is where my heart is.

I attended Honoka'a Elementary, Intermediate, and High School, with a two-year stint at Pahala Elementary from 1975 to 1977. Those dates are seared into my frontal lobe. I recall the bicentennial of our country was the same year our family took our first trip to Disneyland—1976. All four of us Kai kids went with our mom and dad, John and Esther Kai.

Mom was mostly a stay-at-home-mom until we started eating more. Dad was one of the finest police officers on the island, as well as a great high school baseball coach. (Unfortunately, he stopped coaching by the time I got to high school. Otherwise, I would have never been cut from the team!) I would also be remiss if I did not mention that my dad was offered a free-agent contract to play

Without my family in my corner, I would not be here today.

baseball in the Milwaukee Braves farm system, but he turned it down due to his love for my mother. That was an excellent choice because had he chosen to accept the offer, I might not be here and you definitely would not be reading this book!

We had a great upbringing. Mom and Dad did a fine job of raising my oldest brother, Keoni, my younger sister, Elissa, my youngest brother, Len, and myself. We were all two years apart. I got Keoni's hand-me-downs, which I loved because he had great taste. I am proud of every one of my siblings and their individual accomplishments, and I love and honor my parents. I am so glad they stuck it out through thick and thin and are still together to this day after forty-plus years of marriage. Without my family in my corner, I would not be here today.

I'm sure my wife, Lisa, never thought she would become a Christian—coming from a strong Buddhist background and household—let alone marry a pastor. Lisa's childhood home included an entire wall dedicated to her parents' Buddhist faith. Displayed were portraits, figurines, and paintings of young smiley-faced Chinese children with rosy cheeks, pure white skin, and lollipops in their hands. As a baby, Lisa was dedicated to become a monk. However, she had other plans, which is a good thing. She would not look good at all with a shaved head and a black robe.

CHURCH ROOTS

Although my roots were established in the Catholic faith, Hope Chapel is the only contemporary church I have ever known. In fact, I gave my life to Jesus at a Hope Chapel in 1989 in Kane'ohe, Hawai'i. Hope Chapel is a movement of approximately 700 churches of varying sizes and styles scattered throughout the world. Most of the Hope Chapels in Hawai'i are members of the International Church of the Foursquare Gospel, a denomination whose headquarters are situated in Los Angeles, California. You might be familiar with some of our contemporary denominational leaders, including Jack Hayford, Ralph Moore, and Wayne Cordeiro. Founded by Aimee Semple McPherson in the 1920s, Foursquare has almost 60,000 churches in over 144 countries and 1,800 churches in the United States.[1]

LISA

Lisa and I have had the privilege and honor of pastoring Hope Chapel West O'ahu since 2001. My mentor, Ralph Moore, one of the greatest church-planters in the world today, discipled me two years after I got saved because he wanted to make sure that Lisa Lum (with whom I'd become smitten and would become my wife of nineteen years at this writing) was not dating an ax murderer. Why? Because when Lisa and I met, I was a divorced single-dad. Lisa and I dated, got serious, broke up, and kept our "just friends" status for a year. We had an agreement to not talk to one another in order to see if love would rekindle. I did not keep my end of the agreement, because I realized that I did not want to live without her. So, we were eventually reunited and in three months we were married.

Before meeting Lisa, I prayed and asked God that if I were to marry again, to please lead a five-foot-seven drop-dead gorgeous Asian woman my way. Yes, Asian. Listening to pastor Jack Hayford on the radio one day, I heard him say we should be specific in our prayers. So, that is what I was—specific. On that day, I added further specifications to my prayer and asked that if He did bring me a woman with those attributes who would eventually become my wife, to make sure she loved Jesus more than she loved me. That way, I would know for sure she would never leave me. Well, as you know by now, God did more than deliver! People who know Lisa say they notice both an innocence and a regalness about her. She is not stuck-up, by any stretch of the imagination, but instead carries herself with an inner confidence that only comes from spending time with God. I also need to add that, at twenty-one, Lisa was a runner-up for the Miss Chinatown pageant. Not too shabby, huh?

Lisa and I met after I had been attending Hope Chapel for about a year. Because I had to wake up early to take care of my then two-year-old daughter, Courtney, I was going to the Sunday morning eight o'clock services. There was a Friday evening young adult service, but I never felt up for a "singles service." Besides, I usually worked Friday nights at a restaurant, earning about a hundred dollars in tips as a valet.

After a while, my best friend, Brandon, who worked with me at the restaurant and brought me to Hope Chapel, convinced me to sign up for the singles ministry Christmas party. I was reluctant. I was not ready for Christian dating, and, honestly, for some reason I did not think Christian women were good-looking. Serious! How wrong I was! There were wall-to-wall attractive, single Christian women. But before I could thank Brandon for getting this "old codger" out of the house and to the party, my eyes set upon one particularly fine, young woman. Lisa was sitting at the registration table, signing in guests before they entered the banquet hall. I tried playing it cool, but some unspoken chemistry kept flying between the young lady and myself. I went in with Brandon, and my old nightclub ways, although much more sanctified, began to come back to me. I was actually enjoying myself. The evening came to an end, and, lo and behold, we happened to meet up with Lisa and her friends at Zippy's, a local restaurant.

The following day my phone rang and I picked it up. On the other end of the line I heard, "Hi. This is Lisa. Remember me from last night?" I said, "Oh! Sure I remember you. How are you?" After telling me she was fine (and I would add, *in more ways than one, Honey!*), she proceeded to ask me out on a date. "I was wondering if you'd like to accompany me to my best friend's wedding. It's next weekend, but the thing is, I'm in the wedding party so you'd be sitting with some of my friends. Is that okay?" I was a little taken aback because, I thought, one, *this girl doesn't waste any time* (I would later discover that because she worked in the singles department at church she had access to the roster and my phone number!). Two, I had never been on a date where I would not be sitting

He must have been thinking, *Who is this player? What a loser.*

with the one I was dating. And three, I was usually the one asking someone out, not the other way around. After the initial shock wore off, I told Lisa I thought I was available, thumbed through my day planner loud enough for her to hear, then made arrangements to be there. In actuality, I was really excited to see her. She fit my prayer to a T!

Saturday morning could not have come sooner. I drove to an unfamiliar part of the island, and when I arrived at the church, would you believe, the clutch on my 1982 Datsun B210 broke. What terrible timing. Pastor Ralph, who just happened to be standing outside, took a look at my car and noticed I was having some trouble. He must have been thinking, *Who is this player? What a loser.* I was so embarrassed. I forget what happened to the car that day, or how I got to the reception.

When Lisa and I started dating, she was working part-time for Hope Chapel Kane'ohe as a young adults ministry administrator and at the Shiseido makeup counter at a department store. In addition to being a valet at a restaurant called The Willows, I also was employed on the ramp at American Airlines and had my own multi-level marketing business.

So after the whole dating, break-up, reunited routine, Lisa and I got married on September 25, 1993, by Pastor Ralph. I had clearly passed the "Ralph Test" and he approved of me and of our marriage. Little did I know the role this man would play in my future.

NOT YOUR TYPICAL WEDDING

We got married in record time and were now joined together in holy matrimony. We wanted to begin our future as soon as possible—me, Lisa, and Courtney, an instant blended family. After the life I had before, I was amazed to be given another chance.

Just as the last guests began filtering out of the reception hall, I was about to step off the stage with Lisa when the unthinkable occurred. Pastor Ralph came up to me, stuck his finger in my chest, and said, "You ought to be a pastor!" I was shocked. Trust me when I say it almost ruined my honeymoon. Why? Because I did not want to be a pastor. I wanted to be a millionaire! And if I'm

God was arranging this marriage for something greater than I understood at the time.

a pastor, I reasoned, I can't be a millionaire. Even more disturbing, I knew deep-down that God was calling me. And Ralph coming up to me at that moment confirmed my fears that it would eventually happen. I guess he had heard earlier times when I would sing and joke around from the podium. Perhaps he also had heard about the fruit God was producing in me as a volunteer at Hope Chapel Kane'ohe. Not to mention, I was marrying the woman many considered to be "Miss Hope Chapel." By the time we married, Lisa had become the children's ministry director.

Today, I look back and remember the days leading up to the proposal. I am now convinced it was an arranged marriage. Not the kind where a picture-bride from the mother country is sent to a young man making his way in America. No, it's as though God was arranging this marriage for something greater than I understood at the time. But now it's so much clearer to me. God was bringing us together not just because we loved one another deeply, but for a greater purpose. One that becomes clearer year after year. Lisa has been, and continues to be, the most important person in my corner, next to Jesus.

In the ensuing years, we had our early struggles like any couple, and we also endured the stresses of a blended family. For a while we decided to wait on having more children. Within a few years, the Lord would bless us with Rebekah and nine years later, Charis.

MAKING THE MOST OF YOUR "CORNER PEOPLE"

I am so grateful for the people in my corner. Every boxer has a trainer and a cut-man. The trainer is the main man in the fighter's corner. He yells encouragement, caution, and the occasional rant to guide and motivate him. The trainer doesn't just appear at fight time. He is involved every step of the way, from practice, to road-work (conditioning), and to sparring. He is in charge of the fighter's diet and sleep. He is a guardian for the fighter, and without a trainer, a fighter's days are numbered.

There are times when a trainer has to push and even bring correction to the one he is training. Years ago, when still on staff at Hope Chapel Kane'ohe Bay (HCKB), two other junior staff members and I were asked by a department leader to do a task for him. In essence, he was delegating his responsibilities to those of us who didn't work in his department. As we were trained to understand it, delegation normally worked from the top down. In other words, you build your own teams and you delegate certain responsibilities to your team members. This situation, I argued, was delegating laterally. "You need to build your own team," I protested. "I'm not going to wake up at five in the morning to set up the bookstore when you can do it yourself. Besides, I already wake up at four, four days a week to work my other job at American Airlines, so you are crazy if you think. . . ." My mouth runneth over. It wouldn't have been so bad if this conversation had taken place in private with just the four of us. The problem was, it took place in public (a sandwich shop), in front of other colleagues (fourteen more members of the staff), and in front of my superiors (Pastor Ralph, aka my "trainer" and mentor).

How I wish I could have stopped myself before I had so easily done the "open mouth, insert foot" routine. Ralph leaned over from the other booth and everyone leaned away. He looked at me and said, "You're going to set that bookstore up until Jesus returns." The sandwich shop suddenly went quiet. I'm sure some of what happened will go down in Hope Chapel folklore, but this was definitely one of those moments where I needed to be corrected and disciplined, just like a trainer would to the one he's training. Just recently Ralph was part of our church service and we publicly recalled the incident and had a laugh. But then he got serious and told everyone, "The reason I did that was because the Michael Kai I knew, who would drive in a leaky old Jeep Cherokee and do anything and anytime, was in danger of losing his way." Addressing the congregation, he continued, "He was not living up to the Michael I knew and hired—he was operating below it. I needed to get his attention and get him back." Thank God for trainers.

Another person you'll need in your corner is a cut-man. This person is the one who patches up the fighter during a boxing match as the trainer coaches him between rounds. He ices down his bruised face and stops the bleeding from his eyebrow. Throughout a boxing match, the fighter is subject to a varying

•∞•

Who do you have in your corner that examines your conditon and patches you up?

•∞•

array of punches (upper-cut, left hook, right jab), landing in varying places on the body (head, ribs, groin). By the fifth round, a boxer is beat and bloodied, his chest heaving for every ounce of oxygen he can inhale. When the bell announces the next round, boxer, trainer, and cut-man will reunite again in a few minutes for more of the same. After the coaching and medical attention, he launches you from his stool back to where the enemy awaits. Not only do you need a trainer (mentor), but you also need a cut-man. Who are those cut-men or cut-women in your life? Who do you have in your corner that examines your condition and patches you up? Please know that a great cut-man will not let you nurse your wounds. You'll want to quit at times, but he or she won't let you entertain the thought for very long. This person will pull you off the stool, pat you on the back, kick you out of the corner, and say, "Off you go!"

There have been some key people in my corner who have filled that role in one season or another. Aaron Suzuki is one. Aaron came over with Ralph from California in the early '80s to start the first Hope Chapel in Hawai'i. He was on staff at HCKB while I was there and even did our pre-marital counseling. He was a huge help to us back then and still is to this day.

Ecclesiastes 4:12 says, "Though one may be overpowered, two can defend themselves. A cord of three strands is not quickly broken." Christian brothers and sisters are better together. It sounds like a cliché, but it's true. We need each other and there are others who need you. We bring wise counsel and encourage each other. My family was in my corner in my early years. The toughest, most painful years of my life happened prior to coming to Jesus. And if it were not for the sacrifices of my mother and father, I shudder to think where Courtney and I would be today and who we would've become. In fact, my entire family readjusted their lives to help me succeed and get through the pain and abandonment that both Courtney and I endured. I am so grateful to them. I tear up just writing this.

Yes, I am thankful for the people in my corner. Who do you have in yours? If you've got what I have been describing, you know how good it is. If you don't, let me offer some advice. First, make sure you bring in the right people. If you look around, you will likely find them. One of the best things we can do to assemble trusted corner people is to first be a friend (Proverbs 18:24). You will want people who have the right chemistry with you, people who you "click" with. Additionally, you'll want to have people with the right character because who they are in their private life must reflect their public life. If these are the ones who will be advising you and speaking into your life, you'll want to make sure what is being imparted to you is of solid substance.

I'm sure you could come up with a few more qualities you'd like to have in your corner, but the most important thing to do will be to pray for the right people. Also, it's important to note that different seasons will bring different people into your corner. Those who were in my corner ten years ago are not the same as those today. There will be a role and a time for those in your corner as people will come and go. Some will be there for a long time, like the prophet Samuel was for David (1 Samuel 16:1–13, 19:18–24). Samuel officiated over David's first anointing service when David was still shepherding sheep as a teen.

When one person leaves your corner, the Lord often provides another who will take his or her place.

He was also present into David's early adulthood and a confidante until his death (1 Samuel 25:1). When one person leaves your corner, the Lord often provides another who will take his or her place when their season is over. Nathan, another prophet, filled that role later in David's adulthood after he was crowned King of Israel (2 Samuel 7:1–17, 2 Samuel 12:1–14). Additionally, Zadok and Abiathar, both priests, as well as the prophet Gad, played similar roles in the lifetime of David.

Most important of all, remember that the Lord knows who you'll need when you need it. Keep praying and keep your eyes open, and you'll discover them.

---

[1] *The History of the Foursquare Church*. www.foursquare.org/about/history (2011).

CHAPTER 4

THE MAKING OF A PRIZEFIGHTER

The Early Lessons of Faithfulness

"Again, it will be like a man going on a journey, who called his servants
and entrusted his wealth to them. To one he gave five bags of gold,
to another two bags, and to another one bag, each
according to his ability. Then he went on his journey."

Matthew 25:14–15

Trust is an important element in our relationship with Jesus. Think about it. We've been entrusted with gifts, talents, finances, relationships, material possessions, and the like. Jesus has entrusted Lisa and me with His Bride, the Church, and more specifically, Hope Chapel West O'ahu. He has trusted us with the lives of people, the health of His flock, the stewardship of finances, the dreams and goals of people, and so on. And "*to whom much is given, much is required.*" Since I've been given much, much will be required of me. It also means there will be an accounting to determine what you and I have done with what was entrusted to us.

If you're in a position of leadership, you've been *entrusted* with leading your people, business, or organization with fairness and integrity. If you are on the worship team and sing or play an instrument, you've been entrusted with a gift to lead people into the presence of the Lord, and required to steward the gift He's given you with integrity of heart and skillfulness of hands (Psalm 78:72). If you've been given the ability to build businesses, earn a profit, and have been blessed with entrepreneurial skills, you've been *entrusted* with a gift that allows you to enjoy the fruits of your labor. But you are also *required* to extend a helping hand financially, or to perhaps teach others so that God's

✿

If you've been given, if you've been entrusted, more is required.

✿

Kingdom can be expanded in the marketplace. In Luke 12:48 (NLT), Jesus said, "When someone has been given much, much will be required in return; and when someone has been entrusted with much, even more will be required." Did you see that? Given, required. Entrusted, required. There's a cause and an effect. If you've been given, if you've been entrusted, more is required.

There is a difference between what we are given and what is entrusted to us. For example, God has given us the bodies we have. Even though it is a free gift, there is an amount of stewardship involved. If I quit taking care of my body, God may not take it away from me but there will eventually be consequences (health issues). It is up to me what I do with what I've been given.

When we are entrusted with something, it appears to be something that is dear to the Lord's heart. For example, we are entrusted with relationships. If we quit investing in those relationships, we could lose them. If you are entrusted with His Bride, the Church, your responsibility is to steward it well. If not, it could be taken from you and given to another.

Take a good look around you. Look closely and you will see all that you have been given. I don't think there's anyone who can honestly say that they haven't been given a thing. Got children? A job? A bus pass? A stomachache? Then you have been given something! (Just kidding about the stomachache.)

Some other things Jesus gives us are free, like grace and salvation. Grace and salvation have nothing to do with my previous performance or track record, nor with how good or bad I have been. Why? Because grace and salvation cannot be earned. Paul writes, "For the wages of sin is death, but the free gift of God is eternal life through Christ Jesus our Lord" (Romans 6:23 NLT). The free gift given to us is salvation, which we do not contribute a single thing to. Why? Because it is free and you can't earn something you've been freely given. In fact, I saw a tweet quoting William Temple, "The only thing we contribute to salvation is the sin that makes it necessary."

You might be thinking, *I haven't been given much. I've had to earn and scratch to attain everything I have.* You might think you are self-made, but the truth is that without God, you could not have done what you have accomplished. Deuteronomy 8:18 says, "But remember the Lord your God, for it is he who gives you the ability to produce wealth."

We are not entrusted with something until we have proven that we can be.

Although you have been able to do what you do, God now raises the stakes and takes the "given" to the next level, "entrust." Because of your trustworthiness in what you have been given, you will now move to the level of being entrusted with the things near to God's heart. To be trustworthy is to be deserving of confidence; someone who is dependable or reliable. At this very moment, you are proving whether you can be reliable and trustworthy. You see, we are not entrusted with something until we have proven that we can be.

For example, before my dad allowed me to drive the car on the weekends, I had to prove to him first that I knew how to drive safely. Second, I needed to prove I would return the car in good condition and help with its maintenance. Because I was a good driver and treated the car as if it were my own, I was never restricted from using the car. If I had ever returned the car with an empty gas tank, or dirty and scratched, my dad would not find me trustworthy and would not allow me to use it for a while. But because I had a previous track record of trustworthiness with his car, I earned the privilege of using it again and again, for as long as I lived up to the set agreement.

I see two things happening here. The first is you will be "given" something. But notice there is a second step in operation; what follows next is being *entrusted* with something else. Yes, Jesus said, "To whom much is given, much is required," but in essence, He raises the stakes and says, "To whom much has been entrusted, *even more* will be required."

The Greek word for "given" is *didomi. Didomi* is translated as to *give something to someone of one's own accord, to bestow or furnish.* Something has been provided to and *for you* in order that something might be put to use through you. So you and I have been provided with something. *Didomi.*

The next level happens when you have been entrusted with something. Did you catch that the something, whatever it may be, is not yours? It belongs to someone else. This means to "commit to one's charge, to deposit." I have been given much, and much has been bestowed upon me. It is a gift. *Didomi.* And because much has been *didomi* to Michael, much will be required of me. "Much" in the Greek is the word *poly,* as in *many.* The next word in the New King James Version is translated as "more," which you and I can agree is greater than "much." "More" in the Greek is *perissoteros,* or *"over and above, more than is necessary, superadded, exceeding abundantly, supremely."* Did you see that? If you've been given much, much will be required of you. But if you've been entrusted, committed or deposited with much, mega-more will be required of you!

Furthermore, the word "required" is also translated as *"demanded."* To whom much is given, much is demanded. But we aren't done. There's more. The operative, deal-breaker word in this verse is to me the word "whom." That's me. That's you. And this is where the responsibility of the *whom* is being placed.

In my humble estimation, Jesus is placing all the responsibility on you and me for everything He has given as well as entrusted to us. No matter what amount we have been given, an adequate amount, a mustard seed-sized amount, or much, it is our responsibility to steward it. And if we have the privilege of being "entrusted" with something (leadership, money, people, time), mega-more or poly-more will be demanded from us in return. Wow. Let that one sink in for a minute.

So let me ask you this question: What are you doing with what you've got?

On the Way From Self-Made God To God-Made

Early on, I learned two lessons as a kid: money doesn't grow on trees (you need to work hard) and faithfulness is vital. Each time my parents doled out our allowance, I thought, *This isn't going to last me very long*. Don't get me wrong, I was grateful. But I also knew there was fierce competition in my home, and I learned that just because you did the same amount of work, it didn't mean you got the same amount of pay. Similar to the parable of the talents, we are not given what we thought we deserved. Case in point: Keoni had me beat by two years, one month, and twenty-two days. Though he may have been slightly taller than me, we did essentially the same amount of chores at home. One week he would mow the lawn, the next week I would. One week he would wash the cars, the next week I did. But when mom lined us all up to give us our allowance, Keoni got an Andrew Jackson, a twenty-dollar bill, while I, doing the same amount of chores (at a much superior level of workmanship, I might add) got an Alexander Hamilton, a ten-dollar bill! I quickly realized we don't all get what we think we're worth.

That started me on a journey of earning my own money. What motivated me was my expensive taste in basketball shoes. The Kais were not wealthy. Growing up, I overheard my parents engaged in vigorous, robust discussions about finances and how to stretch a dollar. So I never prompted my parents for more money because I didn't want to burden them. I decided that if I were to satisfy my desire to look good and feel good, then I would have to get out there and get a job, at the illegal age of ten.

I had all kinds of jobs growing up. I picked macadamia nuts at twenty-five cents per five-gallon bucket. That lasted two weeks. Then I tried babysitting. I was actually pretty good with the compliant kids, and when word got around, I was getting calls. It was a piece of cake! It was exciting starting a cottage industry at the young age of eleven, even before there was such a term! Until one day, a young couple with a two-year-old and a four-year-old heard about Michael Kai's highly rated babysitting services. My mom dropped me off at their home, I received some quick instructions, and off went the young couple to their party while I fully expected this would be an evening of easy money—like taking candy from, well, a baby.

What's an eleven-year-old boy doing babysitting little kids anyway?

Boy, was I wrong! Nothing that night went as planned. Those two little boys were out-of-control. Looking at the clock every ten minutes, I was literally on the verge of a mental breakdown. That's when it hit me: I didn't need this. What's an eleven-year-old boy doing babysitting little kids anyway? *Girls are supposed to do this*, I thought to myself. So, needless to say that was the end of my budding cottage industry.

A couple of jobs later, Keoni decided he wanted to take a break from his paper route. So, I picked up his route. I learned how to fold the papers and stuff them into the canvas bag emblazoned on the front with "Hawai'i Tribune Herald." The advantage to this job was the thirty dollars I would be earning for one month's work. That was big money! But it was also really hard work. Every afternoon, right after school, I picked up that bag stuffed with 150 newspapers and took off on my bike. For over a mile, I'd ride down a hazardous highway called the Hawai'i Belt Road, a two-lane highway where semi trucks and tour buses whizzed by at sixty miles an hour. I pedaled my yellow, two-wheel, banana-seat bike up a steady grade incline until I reached the top of the climb, then I slowly began my descent, delivering my papers with professionalism and excellence. That lasted about a month. Then Keoni took back his route.

Although none of these jobs were long-term commitments, they definitely taught me the value of a dollar. But more importantly, the spiritual values of faithfulness and fruitfulness were being forged in the formative years of my life. These opportunities for personal growth were being taught to me far before I would surrender my self-made life and exchange it for a God-made life. The lessons I learned carried me during the years of my separation; the season of my life before I gave my life to Jesus.

STEPPING INTO THE RING

The problem was, my early experiences in earning my way gave me a false impression of having my way. When you feel you have paid the price and have earned what you have, there is a tendency to think you are entitled to having things your way. I fell into this trap. The tenacity I had developed as a strength was now in danger of becoming my weakness. I can only imagine what kind of

The tenacity I had developed as a strength was now in danger of becoming my weakness.

life I would be living if I hadn't obeyed the Lord's call on my life. If I had gone my own way, decided on doing my version of what was best for me, I would definitely not be as fulfilled as I am today. Obedience has its advantages.

Lisa and I had been married for less than a year when I began to feel a strong pull toward leaving my ideas of what I wanted to do with my life. As I mentioned, in addition to working my two jobs I was also involved in multi-level marketing (MLM). Despite how others may feel about it, my experience in MLM proved invaluable. For one thing, I learned the value of reading. I had rarely read a book until then. Today, I love reading. Additionally, I learned public speaking and more importantly, I developed a go-getter attitude that helps to this day.

I tried to put my original MLM plans on the altar. However, there was one problem. While the Lord pulled and led me in one direction, I resisted and leaned in another. Still very involved in my MLM business, I could not break free. I had spent five long years striving and stretching to make the business work, and I honestly thought I should have had more success. I was diligent and hardworking and thought I knew what I was doing. I would look around and blame anything and anyone for my lack of progress. I would blame my wife, my family, even my dog!

In frustration I would journal, crying out to God, "Lord, why am I not moving forward? I'm doing everything everyone else is doing and more! Why is this not happening like I want it to?" I tried to keep a positive outlook, but despite all my activity and efforts, I was stuck in the same place with the same boring view. I was running on a treadmill called "The Fast Track to Success." Ironically, during this time, my heart began to grow for the ministry and the things of God. My desire to serve God and His people gripped me even while I tried to work my business plans harder and harder. I was in a tug-of-war between my desires and His plans.

Eventually, I discovered it's useless fighting against God. In fact, I believe the most unfulfilled Christians are the ones who know God is calling them to a new season or to a new level in life but run away from the calling. It is called disobedience, and that's exactly what I was doing. God, in His mercy and grace, continued to bless me in some ways, but I still tried to have things my own way. C. S. Lewis once said, "There are two kinds of people: those who say to God, 'Thy will be done,' and those to whom God says, 'All right, then, have it your way.'"[1] I was the latter group. I continued to have it my way. I treated my will and His plans like I was pulling up to the drive-through counter at Burger King, with the old 1970s commercial playing in the background: *"Hold the pickles, hold the lettuce, special orders don't upset us . . . have it your way!"* I was set on having it my way while still praying, "Oh, and Lord, please bless my plans!" Remaining disobedient to the Lord, doing *my own thing*, while asking Him to bless my plans was not going to happen. The Lord would have none of it. I would soon discover that never works. And, I was seriously unfulfilled.

Leaving MLM behind wasn't easy. Although the thought of leaving was painful, making the decision to leave was quite simple for me. Circumstances within the organization and the integrity in which they were handled became too much for me to just sit and do nothing about it. It would be the equivalent of someone working in a place where they did not agree with its practices yet still showed up for work and received a paycheck. There was a huge conflict in my heart and I decided that I would not compromise my values. It was clear to me that it was time to leave. Within a few days, I was finished and left my MLM business.

It was easier said than done. I began having withdrawal symptoms. I started feeling insecure about what people still in the business were thinking of me. I was missing the relationships I had developed over five years. I was anxious. In hindsight, I could see that the Lord allowed these circumstances to occur to make me come to a decision. I drew closer to the Lord during this time like I

❧

Although leaving was trying, the future was promising.

❧

had not done in a while. Although leaving was trying, the future was promising. The difficulty I experienced after I left made me realize that I was in bondage to the business I left behind.

THE STICKING POINT

You might be thinking, *Bondage? That's a little strong, isn't it, Mike?* My answer is a straight up, Nope! Here's why: If there is anything in your life that keeps you from answering the call of God and you are unwilling to part ways with it, it has become your master and you are no longer in control. Whatever dominates your time, your thinking, your money, or your heart has become your master. You are being held in bondage to it.

It's simple. If you have a boyfriend or girlfriend you can't break up with and you know you should, or if you can't stop thinking about him or her and you know you've got to get them out of your mind, until you are free from him or her, you are in bondage. If you are spending money on pornography, if it is affecting your desire and your intimacy with your spouse, or has caused you to operate in sexual relationships outside of the covenant of God, you are in bondage. Why? Because if you can't quit, you are enslaved. God calls this sin. It doesn't have to be a substance or a person. It could be a profession, a business, a mindset, or a philosophy. Anything that stands in the way of God is *directly opposed to God*, and it must come to an end. You will have withdrawals. You will crave it in the early stages, but if you can get past that sticking point, you will have victory and the life you were called to live.

I make the occasional visit to the weight room to steward the body the Lord gave me. There was a time in my life when "maxing out" on the bench press was important to me. That is no longer the case. But when it was important, there would always come a time in the workout, usually on the third set, when I would need the help of a friend. Whenever I couldn't lift the weights higher than I needed to, someone would "spot" me, standing behind the bench, offering help while encouraging me to push. This is called the sticking point. You can't get beyond this point without the help of a friend. But with their help, the bar can be brought to its original position. Without help, it would come crashing down on your neck or chest causing great damage. With help, you have pushed your muscles to the max, thereby conditioning them to break past the sticking point in future workouts. My sticking point was my MLM business. Get past the sticking point and you will reach a level you never thought you could.

The happiest, most fulfilled people on the face of this planet are those who are doing what they were called to do. They are the most joyful people because they are experiencing the pleasure and favor of God in their lives. Do you see yourself in this category of people? Or have you run away from your calling? When I finally left my plans behind, when I finally pushed past the sticking point, God began working in my life in greater ways than ever before.

THE HONEYMOONERS

When I first joined the staff at Hope Chapel Kane'ohe Bay, I reported directly to Rob McWilliams, who today is one of my closest friends. Ralph hired me, but Rob spent day-to-day time with me. Ralph discipled me, but Rob mentored me daily. I was not brought on staff because I had a Bible college or seminary degree. The Lord called me, while I was busy doing *something*, which was faithfully ushering at church on the weekends and serving as a MiniChurch (small groups) shepherd or overseer. I was faithful in these ministry assignments, and they were producing fruit. This caught the eye of the leaders around me.

41

When I joined the staff at HCKB, I was given (there's that word) the chance to create The Honeymooners, a new ministry for young-married couples. I was so grateful to be on the team, living the dream as a "pastoral assistant." (I tried getting Rob to change my title to assistant pastor, but he said they were already stretching it with the current title.) Working alongside my new bride and partner in life, Lisa, I went to work building this new ministry. I organized camps and dances. But more importantly, I rallied together two MiniChurches, multiplying those two to make four, and then those four to become eight, and so on. By the time the Lord had called me out of The Honeymooners, we had ten

There are things that go through your mind when your boss says he wants to go for a walk with you.

MiniChurches, and I had a lot of fun in the process. This exercise of small group multiplication would be woven into our DNA at Hope Chapel West O'ahu. Things were going well and everyone was happy. Then, I took a walk that would change my life.

A Short Walk in a Long Direction

After coordinating The Honeymooners ministry, Ralph approached me one Sunday at church between services. "Let's take a walk," he said. I was really nervous. There are things that go through your mind when your boss says he wants to go for a walk with you. Hmm? Reprimand? Hmm. Is he going to do "The Donald" (as in Trump) on me?

"I need you to take over the youth ministry," he finally said. I had a feeling this was coming. I was not looking to become a youth pastor. I couldn't stand high school kids. They were immature, selfish, and annoying. But by now God began stirring in me thoughts about someday becoming a senior pastor. The Lord began to show me over and over again that if I was faithful with a few,

42

faithful with whatever He gave me, He'd put me in charge of much more. So, I said yes to God's call to become a youth pastor.

Looking back on my days as a youth pastor, I have to say that I enjoyed every minute of it. I absolutely loved preaching to the youth, I loved the fruit that resulted from retreats and seeing students give their lives to Jesus. Being a youth pastor was like running a church without all the responsibility of a senior pastor. I learned so much in those four years as a youth pastor at HCKB. Pastor Ralph trusted me, no, he *entrusted* me with the lives of the next generation in a great church.

I came to love what I was doing for the Lord. The ministry that I wasn't fond of leading had become one of the passions of my life. When I took over the youth department, I poured myself into the role of equipping and empowering the next generation. It was hard work, yet very rewarding. I drew great satisfaction knowing I was faithful to what the Lord entrusted to me. Then, after five fruitful years, in the midst of my faithfulness, God did something. It was like he threw a curveball that would leave me wondering what would happen in the future.

A GLIMPSE OF THE FUTURE

Up until 1999, I had never met a prophet nor was I interested in receiving a prophetic word. I had a limited understanding of the gift or the function of a prophet. Although I come from a Pentecostal denomination, at the time, I wasn't as savvy in the area of the Holy Spirit as I am today.

It wouldn't be fair of me to say that I never saw it happen because I had seen it at a convention, mostly from afar. I had experienced great words of encouragement, and sometimes someone would have a word of knowledge for me. It was usually Pastor Ralph. But as far as someone who had a prophecy for me? Nah.

Lisa and I flew to the Big Island, along with some of the Hope Chapel staff, for an International Church of the Foursquare Gospel (ICFG) Northwest District conference. As I mentioned earlier, ICFG was founded by one of the most amazing and influential women in the history of the United States, the late Aimee Semple McPherson. "Sister Aimee," as she was affectionately called, was an anointed and powerful evangelist in the '20s and '30s who traveled throughout the U.S. conducting tent revivals. She would pack up a tent in her car and drive from one town to the next, as the Holy Spirit directed. Thousands of men and women surrendered their lives to Jesus through her evangelistic and healing tent meetings. Eventually, she settled in the Echo Park area of Los Angeles. Then, in the middle of the darkest Depression years, Sister Aimee accomplished the impossible by building the Angeles Temple, which seats 5,000 to this day. Her services were so innovative that Hollywood insiders would sneak in to witness her illustrated sermons in order to get ideas. You may recall hearing the old song, "Hurray for Hollywood." Listen closely and you'll hear her name being sung after the name "Shirley Temple." She truly was a pioneer sustaining and building a church through the Great Depression.

The Lord used His daughter, Sister Aimee, to send out missionaries and church planters all across the world. In the state of Hawai'i, Foursquare Churches (which include the New Hope Christian Fellowship churches pastored by Wayne Cordeiro, and the Hope Chapel churches, pastored by Ralph Moore) are some of the most prevalent Charismatic-Pentecostal churches.

At the conference we attended was a prophet named Jean Darnall. We were invited to sit with Sister Jean in a room with five other couples. We sat down in front of her. To one side of our little group was a secretary with a tape recorder. Before Sister Jean even began to speak, I was afraid of what was going to come

❧
Who could feel threatened by some sweet old lady?
❧

out of her mouth. At the same time, I was very curious and excited. Up until this point, I was skeptical and a little cynical. All this was birthed out of a lack of understanding. But I soon realized there was no reason to fear. Sister Jean was an old lady by then. Who could feel threatened by some sweet old lady?

She looked at me and uttered something to the effect of, "You can sell ice cream to the Eskimos," and, "I see you standing on a soapbox in a busy intersection with a megaphone in your hand coming from your mouth and the word I am getting is 'amplified or broadcast.'" Then she said, "Tell me, are you on TV or the radio?" I was amazed. She had no idea our youth ministry was on public access television. She "saw" that I was going to be on the radio preaching the Gospel, and it's come true. We have been on the radio for more than a decade now. Not only did she confirm some things that were already in place, but she spoke of things in the future, things that I had no idea we would be blessed to be a part of. We left that room glad that we had entered.

When Lisa and I returned home from the conference we rejoiced over the things that were said about our future. We wondered if this was what Mary felt like when she was told all that she would carry; and like Mary we treasured what was said to us in our hearts.

---

[1] C.S. Lewis, *The Screwtape Letters* (New York: Touchstone, 1943).

CHAPTER 5

MOVING UP IN WEIGHT CLASS

Increasing Your God-Given Capacity

"For not from the east nor from the west nor from the south come promotion and lifting up. But God is the Judge! He puts down one and lifts up another."
Psalm 75:6–7 AMP

When I hear the word *faithful*, I think of a husband who marries the woman of his youth. There has been no other woman in his life, nor will there be. This man and woman will endure and celebrate the different seasons of life together. Together they will raise children, spoil grandchildren, and celebrate their fiftieth anniversary with friends and family.

When I hear the word *faithful*, I imagine a salesman who has worked for over forty years at the same company. He has pounded the pavement and done his best to remain one of the top producers, with an internal engine that keeps him going despite losing a sale or a contract. He changes with the company from the typewriter to floppy disks to Palm Pilots to iPhones. At the end of his career he has passed on trade secrets and wisdom to the up-and-coming young guns. At his retirement party all the employees chip in to buy him an expensive gold watch with an inscription on its back simply stating, "*You Were Faithful.*"

Often, faithfulness is found in places you'd never even bother to look. We see the championship game but not the hours of blood, sweat, and tears of the one practicing on his own, long after everyone has gone home. We see the A+ student giving the Valedictorian speech on graduation day, but not the tutoring she received in the tenth grade, or her saying "no" to things that would distract her

Faithfulness is always followed, eventually, by fruitfulness.

drive to improve. We see the big church with its buildings, technology, and conferences, but what we don't see are the pioneering years of hard work it took just to get the church off of the ground.

That's faithfulness. But faithfulness is never alone. Faithfulness has always got a little brother following close behind. He can't shake it even if he wanted to. Faithfulness is always followed, eventually, by fruitfulness.

All this brings to mind the mango tree. It seems that almost every home I've ever lived in had a mango tree in the backyard. I love mangos. They are sweet, succulent, and best eaten like an apple. Peel away part of the skin and bite into it, while the juice runs down your chin. They are incredibly delicious! But before the mango is harvested it begins as a blossom. The blossom is the beginning stage of the fruit.

As in life and ministry, we can become discouraged when we fail to see fruit in the early stages. But if you look closely you'll be able to identify the blossoms of the beginning stages of fruitfulness. It's predictable. If you see the blossoms then you can expect fruit to follow. Fruitfulness is always preceded by faithfulness.

Some seasons bring a higher yield of fruit than others. Sometimes the mango trees bear more fruit in one season than in previous seasons. One thing we need to keep in mind is that we are not in charge of the amount of fruit we bear. We can control our *faithfulness* but we have no control over the amount of fruit we yield. Keep being faithful to what God called you to do, *and you will bear fruit.*

In this particular season of our lives, little buds of faithfulness were beginning to appear on the tree.

> *"Behold, I am doing a new thing; now it springs forth, do you not perceive it?"*
>
> Isaiah 43:19 ESV

The New Millennium, the year 2000 (Y2K), was a great year of fruitfulness for us in the ministry. Lisa was hitting her full stride in children's ministry. She had done such a great job in recruiting and equipping leaders that all the major tasks were delegated to a very gifted and dedicated team. With Lisa at the helm, the ministry hummed like a well-oiled machine. Pastor Ralph would point out that Lisa had become so adept at recruiting and delegating that he liked to say that by noon every day, she would sit at her desk, filing her nails because everything was running along just fine. Lisa didn't fully agree with the filing her nails part; nevertheless, it was an accurate description of her effectiveness as an equipper.

As for me, I was in the midst of my best year in youth ministry. I felt our team of student and adult leaders was the best when it came to the combination of character and skill. We gelled, kids were going off to colleges on the West Coast, camp numbers were at a record high, and the Holy Spirit was moving in our youth ministry like never before. My secret desire to be a national speaker with Youth Specialties, a youth workers' equipping ministry, began budding in my mind. At least, that was what I was hoping for. However, I was working as a youth pastor in a church where church-planting was what you were likely to do.

DASHBOARD CONFESSIONALS

One Sunday afternoon I drove up the long, steep driveway to the church, and as I was parking the car, I heard the voice of the Holy Spirit speak to me. His voice was not audible; I heard it inside my head. He said, "You won't be here very long." Wow! I don't recall that ever happening to me before, at least not with that kind of clarity. Of course, this naturally made me pause and consider what had just happened. As I turned the engine off, I paused long enough to ponder what had taken place. I stepped out of the car, intending to keep close to me what I had just heard.

However, I knew I could not keep this from Ralph. I had to find him and tell him. I'm so thankful for the relationship we continue to have with Pastor Ralph and Ruby Moore. Lisa and I were privileged to have served on staff for over twenty years combined when we were at HCKB. I am convinced that we received some of the best training and mentoring in the entire state when we were there.

The Moores not only were great examples in church planting and pastoring, but they also became our family outside our parents. Though no one could ever take our parents' place, Ralph and Ruby played a huge role in our lives when my mom and dad moved to Oregon. Lisa's parents, as Buddhists, didn't quite understand what we were doing with the church. They moved to Hawai'i from Hong Kong when she was a a little over a year old, and eventually there would be a total of four children in the Lum household. I have so much admiration and respect for my in-laws. I think it was a shock to their Chinese system when Lisa married a multi-racial guy with a light complexion and a Hawaiian last name. But now I'm sure they love me. After all, I'm the one who introduced hugging to the normally un-physical Lum family. And I am grateful for their raising of the most beautiful woman in Hawai'i just for me.

Ralph and Ruby Moore played the role of surrogate parents in our lives. We even vacationed with them once early in our marriage. My two oldest daughters, Courtney and Rebekah, learned how to swim in their pool. We'd spend every July Fourth at their home and many a Sunday afternoon swimming and

❦

We talked shop constantly, and I was a sponge soaking it all up.

❦

barbecuing. Ralph even taught me how to change the oil in my car. Ralph and I rarely sat down for one-on-one meetings. Most of my discipleship and mentoring took place in the context of weekly staff meetings for seven years (for me), and impromptu meetings in the pool or under the hood of a car. We talked shop constantly. And I was a sponge soaking it all up. I loved every minute of it.

One thing I respected in him was that he never seemed to hide his intentions or plans from me. Even if he was upset or disappointed with me (mainly over something I said), I always knew where he stood. There was no guessing. If you were in the doghouse, you knew your new name was Fido. I appreciated that. There was no jockeying for position, for time, or for attention from him. When you have a boss and mentor like that there's great security and freedom to do what you are called to do. I'm sure some envied the role the Moores played in our lives and the access we had to the boss, but it was more than that. It was a patriarchal friendship that took time to build, and we were grateful for it.

So, as soon as I got out of the car that afternoon, I immediately looked for Ralph. The interesting thing is that it was a Sunday evening and Ralph was rarely ever there on a Sunday night. But this time he was and I found him. When I was able to get his attention, we spent about a minute talking about it.

"Ralph, I think the Lord spoke to me coming up the driveway tonight."

"Really? What'd He say?" he replied.

"He said that I won't be here for very long. Now I don't know what that means. I'm not sure if I'm going somewhere or if I'm moving into the young adults like you thought of doing but that's about it. I thought I needed to tell you. But can you do me a favor and not make any plans for me, I mean, don't rush it?"

"Don't worry. Let's just take it slow and we'll see what the Lord does." And then it was over. That was it. We barely talked about it after that.

JUST WHEN I WAS HAVING FUN

Before I heard "The Voice" I was having the time of my life. It was my fifth year of youth ministry and everything we worked for happened in a big way. In addition to the normal characteristics of a great youth ministry, we had students serving in many of the ministries in the church. Pastor Ralph always appreciated that level of integration into the life of the church. We were taking students to Japan on missions trips and returning with great experiences, all the while sharing the gospel in a nation in which fewer than 1 percent call Him their Lord and Savior.

I look back and fondly recall how at first I didn't want to be a youth pastor. How silly! Those were some of the most fruitful years of my life, but the Lord had other plans for us. He was about to lead us into a new level of faithfulness and fruitfulness.

❧

At first I didn't want to be a youth pastor. How silly!

❧

I didn't rush to make anything happen. I didn't look at every opportunity that came my way as the potential calling for me. I think the biggest reason that I didn't push it was because I loved it there. I loved my job, I loved the people at HCKB, and I loved being a youth pastor. I used to say to Ralph that I had the best job in all of the ministry opportunities in Hawai'i. He agreed. I was having the season of my life! It was July, 2001.

FAITHFULNESS ISN'T JUST ABOUT SHOWING UP

Faithfulness isn't just about showing up, punching in, and punching out. You can hire anybody to do that. Sometimes we view faithfulness as someone standing guard over a wall that is half-built. They make sure that nothing happens to the wall while they're on the clock. It's their "duty" to watch over that wall until someone comes to relieve them from the duty of keeping watch over the wall. That's all they do; show up, on time, to watch over the wall. That's not faithfulness. That's being a watchdog. The average German Shepherd can do that. That's what I call a waste of time, or in our case, "sitting on the talent."

To illustrate this point further, imagine an old man handing off the keys of a church to a young pastor, saying to him, "Here you go, Sonny. Have fun, but don't mess it up. Remember, if it ain't broke, don't fix it. Leave it just the way it is. Don't change a thing, don't fool with nothing, don't rock the boat and by all means, don't upset the apple cart and make the old guard here mad at you. If you heed my warning, it will all work out and then you can hand the keys off to the next guy . . . and give him the same advice."

That's not in me. Mediocrity is something that really frustrates me. Mediocrity, according to my own independent, unabridged dictionary, is as follows: "The best of the worst and the worst of the best." I don't think any of us came into the world one day and said, "Hmmm. When I grow up, I want to be mediocre. I want to just squeak by; just make it." But of course, I could be wrong.

In fact, where did it go wrong? When did we see being faithful as being just "on time"? Could it be because of the uncanny timeliness of the geyser in Yellowstone National Park releasing its sulfuric gasses (and perhaps for marketing purposes) that we began calling it Old Faithful? I understand that particular situation, but is it possible that we see our duties as Christians as being on

Faithfulness is more than just showing up, punching in, and punching out.

time for service, on time for work, on time for everything? I'm all about being on time. I have high standards for our team to show up for everything five minutes early because if you do, you are "on time" in our book. So, faithfulness is more than just showing up, punching in, and punching out.

The Greek word for "faithful," as used in the context of our main Scripture for this book, is the word *pistos*. *Pistos*, when translated into the English vernacular, is defined as a person who shows themselves faithful in the transaction of business, the execution of commands, or the discharge of official duties. See that? The transaction of business would be in the area of profit and loss. Every business or enterprise must show how much profit they made and what their losses were. For a business to be successful, the profits must outweigh the losses. So, you'll surely need someone who is described as "faithful" to operate a business, otherwise you won't be in business very long. Good businessmen are faithful.

Let's look at the execution of commands. Having our servicemen and women of the armed forces at HCWO is an honor. In light of the definition of *pistos* and the "execution of commands," is there anyone more qualified to fill this description than those in the military? I know there are other professions where this is important, such as those in the police force and fire departments, but not many involve life and death and the welfare of many other lives such as those in the military. Good soldiers are faithful.

Let's look at the last one, the "discharge of official duties." This gives us a picture of someone similar to an ambassador of a country, who represents another and speaks on behalf of another and is capable of receiving, delegating, and carrying out the wishes of another. We, as such, are ambassadors for Jesus Christ, carrying out His commands, representing His Kingdom, serving and speaking on behalf of the One we love. Tell me, is this not a huge privilege and responsibility of ours that should be taken seriously? Ambassadors are faithful.

Can you see how one who is faithful is more than the "show-up-and-hold-down-the-fort" type of person? How does faithfulness show up in the life of a student? Simple. You go to class, you are always on time, and you're taking notes and studying them when you have free time. You're a student that (here's a big one for me) is studying for an exam several days in advance and not cramming the evening before. If you take care to be consistent in the little things, you'll be able to perform remarkably well when it comes to the big things (such as exams and finals).

If you're in the ministry, you're not waiting for someone who oversees you to check up on you if you've done your job. YOU hold yourself accountable. YOU don't have to be told what to do. YOU are the one reporting your progress. YOU are the one who is the initiator of pushing for your overseer's time and feedback because it's all on YOU. It's not on your overseer. Don't worry, your overseer is held to the same high standard, both vertically (to his supervisor) and horizontally (to his peers), and in all directions where his leadership is entrusted. You don't have to be told what to do.

INNER CONVICTION

When it comes to being faithful in ministry, the workplace, athletics or academics, this one principle holds true in every aspect of life. Are you ready? Here it is. Don't miss this. You can either operate from inner conviction or you can be operated by external pressure.

You can do things for a variety of good reasons. Either you are motivated by excellence of effort, a personal conviction to do a good job, or by a desire to please the one you are serving. The person who functions from inner conviction is the kind of person I want to work with. These are the kinds of people who have character qualities every employer is looking to hire. I don't know about you but if I have to babysit an employee and keep looking over his shoulder to

You can either operate from inner conviction or you can be operated by external pressure.

see if (a) he's at work; (b) he's doing his job; or (c) he's being productive with the time he is paid for, then I've got the wrong person for the job. However, if this person is ringing the bell on all three and making others around him better for it because of what he brings to the esprit de corps, then that person will continue to move up the charts.

On the other hand, if you are a person who requires external pressure, then you become a burden to those who oversee you. You'll have to be watched to make sure you complete the desired outcomes and expectations that are required for your position. Proverbs 22:29 (NASB) says, "Do you see a man skilled in his work? He will stand before kings; He will not stand before obscure men." Here are a couple of interesting things I've noticed. The Bible quotes this passage as using the phrase, "obscure men." The God's Word Translation refers to the same phrase as "unknown men." So, the reward of someone who is operating out of a personal conviction is one who will rise up to serve in higher levels and with people he or she never thought they would ever partner with! This has proven so true in my life!

54

On another note on Proverbs 22:29, the NASB calls this person we're referring to a "skilled worker." Lest we think this principle is only reserved for someone who falls into the very gifted category, the New Living Translation calls him a "truly competent worker" while the King James refers to him as a "man diligent in his business."

Sometimes I have to stop and be amazed at all the great people the Lord has led Lisa and I to be associated with over the years. To be trained by one of the most fruitful church planters in this generation was a blessing from God. I believe that our diligence, coupled with the sovereignty of God, has brought other relationships into our lives that have benefited us personally, as well as the Kingdom of God. Lest I deceive you into thinking that I've been the perfect student 100 percent of the time in the area of faithfulness and stewardship, I must confess that there've been times when I have failed. But one thing was for sure through those seasons: When I was contributing less than my best, I needed to get out of that funk right away. Because if I "buried the talent" and didn't snap out of it, I would be in danger of losing the talent.

God is calling us to become those in the workplace, marketplace, ministry and every area of life who take what we have and do the best with what we've been given. The man or woman who works hard and makes sacrifices beyond what most people are willing to make—this is the kind of person the Lord elevates. Although it is "man" (your boss, company, division) who carries out the plan, ultimately it is the Lord who promotes you from one level to the next (Psalm 75:6–7). He knows and sees the effort you are putting forth. Nothing that you do is done in vain. Remember, He is a good and just Rewarder.

CHAPTER 6

LET GO OF THE RING

Bidding "Aloha" to What Is Comfortable

"For whoever wants to save their life will lose it,
but whoever loses their life for me and for the gospel will save it."

Mark 8:35

There was something going on in my head, 35,000 feet above sea level. Perhaps it was the combination of the cabin pressure in coach class, the euphoria of being used by God, and having great response at a youth retreat in Eugene, Oregon. Or, maybe it was the envelope I opened while I was flying home from Portland to Honolulu, which contained the honorarium I received from the host church. I had never been paid that much before for ministering at a retreat. Prior to that, whenever I'd spoken at a camp in Hawai'i, I'd get a high-five, a handshake, and a camp T-shirt. Ha! All of it was sweet. I felt like I was in "the zone." Everything was going right. All I know is that I had the time of my life that summer in the outskirts of Eugene.

I was faithful to my calling, at least the calling to be a youth pastor. Yet, I was about to challenge the call of God on my life and could possibly become disobedient to Him. I knew that obedience brought blessing and disobedience would only bring frustration and "kicking against the goads." I knew that if I rebelled against God, all of my efforts as a youth pastor would be met with frustration and futility.

You never win with God that way. *But I was faithful*, I could've argued. *I was doing what He called me to do.* Psalm 37:4 (ESV) says to, "*Delight* yourself in the Lord, and he will give you the desires of your heart." I remember the first time I had done that and the Lord tricked me. I "delighted" in my time with God, and my desires morphed into His desire for me! I wanted what I wanted for me . . . originally. But I was glad it changed to what He wanted.

Now, here I was again, on this roller coaster of emotions between delight and desire. Stuck between two bookends of faith, there was taking joy and delight in Him, forsaking all else, and on the opposite side, was the "desire" part. My desire was to stay. My desire was doing what I wanted to do. What I had been faithful and fruitful at had become my desire. Isn't that the way it's supposed to be?

WHAT SEEMS LIKE A STEP DOWN IS OFTEN A STEP UP

I've heard it said somewhere that God will call you out of your faithful duty to Him. When you're doing what you're called to do, the Master calls you out of your faithfulness and fruitfulness to promote you. What's considered a promotion to some may seem like a demotion to you, but that doesn't matter.

What seems like a step down is often a step up. When I was called to leave HCKB, I initially felt it was a step down. My friend Matt left a very successful

What's considered a promotion to some may seem like a demotion to you.

commercial real estate firm as its vice president and top producer in his region to begin his own company, starting off at the bottom, taking in one-third of the income, scraping his way, so that he could be the boss. He felt the Lord was calling him to it. It's rare that you start at the top. You can take over from some-one, and that's a special privilege in itself, and it's usually given to someone who's been proven to be faithful. But that isn't offered to everyone. Most have to leave what's good to chart their own course.

Abraham had to do the same thing. "Leave your father's home and go to the land that I will show you." There weren't a lot of incentives or bonuses promised for performance. No Abrahamic promise-covenant yet, just "leave." Not even the name of the land, not even a direction on a compass. No East, or "Go West, young man!" Nothing. "Go to the land I will show you," was all He said (Genesis 12:1). Pioneering can be scary!

MEANWHILE BACK AT THE RANCH . . .

I arrived at work the second day after I returned from my trip. It was great to see everyone again. One of the first guys to greet me was Rob McWilliams. "Hey, how you doing? By the way, there's a church that wants you as its pastor. It's in Waikele. They asked me first. I turned them down. So they want to know if you want it. Bye." *Whoa*, I thought, *"What? No—"Hi, hello, how was your time away?" That's it?* That was it. My immediate reaction was, "I'm not interested either." *I'm not going to be someone's consolation prize. I want to be someone's first choice*, I said to myself and went to my office.

If my memory serves me correctly, Pastor Ralph caught me later in the day and mentioned the church opening. He said, "I'd like you to pray about it." In response I said, "No, I don't want to go to Waikele. Besides, it's hot there." For most of the year, that was very true.

The community of Waikele isn't really it's own town. About twenty years ago, Waikele was part of a larger town called Waipahu, predominantly known for its sugarcane fields. In 1995, the Waipahu sugar mill closed.[1] Then one of the largest landowners in Hawai'i decided to develop several hundred acres into a bedroom community that was deemed "affordable housing," an oxy-moron in Hawai'i. They built a large strip mall with homes and townhouses around it and renamed it Waikele. Today the population in Waikele is nearly 15,000.[2]

Pastor Ralph asked me again saying, "No, seriously. Pray about it." To which I replied, "Okay, I'll pray about it." Then, in my smart aleck way, I said, "Okay. I prayed about it. The answer is still no." Pastor Ralph wasn't one to mess around, so he said, "No, I'm serious, Mike. This could be a great opportunity. In fact, I was thinking about going and leaving the church here to you. But, no, I can't leave. Please, Mike. I really want you to consider it."

I explained to him that I didn't have time to pray for another calling. My camp was coming up in a week, I had just returned from Oregon, and there was so much work to be done. But out of deference, I said I'd pray about it. I didn't want to even bother praying about it because I didn't want to go.

At this point, the greatest conflict I had ever come across in five years of full-time ministry was at the forefront of my mind, and I wasn't very thrilled.

Psalm 92:12–13 says, "The righteous will flourish . . . planted in the house of the Lord, they will flourish in the courts of our God." I had been a member of HCKB for twelve years and on staff for over seven years. I was planted there and flourishing there. I wasn't interested in leaving. Everything I had ever known about the ministry, I had learned there. I gave my life to Jesus there, I received my theological training there, and I met and married Lisa there. We

There comes a point when every son has to eventually leave the house.

had our second daughter, Rebekah, while we were there. Under the teaching at HCKB, I learned all the principles about how to steward my finances that allowed me to be able to purchase a home while I was there. I was rooted and definitely planted there. All of our friends were there. Why would we ever want to leave *there?*

Through this experience, I learned even more about what fatherhood meant. There comes a point when every son has to eventually leave the house. In fact, I think it's a joy for a father to equip his son for life, help him determine the best course and chance for success that he could have, and send him on his way to fulfill the calling and destiny the Lord has on his life. As a father to my daughters and to those who I am training and equipping for life and ministry, I feel the same way. There are those who will leave to plant churches, and those who will not leave.

Some will stay and take on an elder-type role much like an uncle or aunt. Their function is much like that of a coach or an assistant coach. They assist in training and counsel, bringing a different approach. Leveraging their influence, they reinforce values, offering a fresh voice and perspective. I can remember the huge roles Rob McWilliams and Aaron Suzuki played in our development. I've seen it happen and am employing the role of "uncles" in our own church today.

THORNS

A mother eagle begins to train her eaglets to fly at a very early stage in their development. She'll take one of the eaglets and put her on her wings. Then she'll fly hundreds of feet in the air on a training mission, and when she suspects she's arrived at an appropriate altitude, she'll suddenly drop the eaglet into thin air. The eaglet's instinct will have to kick in. It will have to make the decision to begin flapping its wings or have a violent introduction to terra firma.

Of course, the eaglet will not learn to fly on its first attempt so its mother will swoop down and catch the eaglet on her back and repeat the same process. When her session with her first eaglet is over, she'll return the freaked out bird to the security of the nest and grab another one of the eaglets for the same lesson. As soon as possible, eaglets are prepared to leave the nest.

But the lesson doesn't end there. She trains them how to hunt and how to receive food she brings to the nest. But one of the most important lessons an eaglet will learn is a shocking one. After one of their test flights, an eaglet will come back to the nest only to discover thorns are in its nest. These thorns keep it from coming back to roost there. The eaglet has become too big, eats too much and more importantly knows too much! It knows too much to remain in the nest. If it were to remain in the nest much longer it would become too dependent on its mother.

Talk about sending a message! Suddenly, the eaglet can no longer return and quickly has to face the fact that it is on its own. Readied, trained and equipped, this eaglet will learn to become an eagle that hunts for its own food, builds its own nest, and will soon find a mate and teach its young how to repeat the process.

I can honestly say that I felt as if Ralph was placing thorns in the nest. I began wondering if he was making room for his son, Carl. Coincidentally, Carl was scheduled to speak at my youth camp that following week. Carl was the quintessential surfer from Huntington Beach (HB), California, living a great life with his wife, Kanani, and witnessing great fruit in HB. It was perfect for him. After graduating from Life Bible College in San Dimas, California, Carl and Kanani pastored a great youth ministry at Hope Chapel Huntington Beach. He was handsome, an incredible surfer, and a great youth pastor. My insecurities got the best of me and I began wondering if I was being set up by the boss. Of course, I understood that Pastor Ralph could make any moves he wanted to

It looked like a thorn was being placed in the nest.

make. Why? Because, I knew he sought the Lord on every major decision and he was the boss. Besides, he had pioneered the church and Carl was just one of the many great leaders Ralph had sent out over the years, and Carl just happened to be his son.

It looked like a thorn was being placed in the nest. Yet I also knew that if I didn't hear from the Lord, Ralph would never force me out sooner than I needed to be. That would be a bad move on everyone's part. During this short period of time, I became more familiar with the sovereignty of God—that even if I had to leave sooner than I would have liked, God would still have my back and work all things together for good (Romans 8:28).

Camp was fast approaching. That next Sunday I was hanging out with students in the church courtyard prior to the start of our youth service. I never liked preparing a sermon before the week of camp. It would be too much stress to add to my camp preparation duties. So, I decided to have a good friend of mine, Jeff MacKay, speak that evening. Jeff's a pastor in Osaka, Japan, and one of the craziest church planters I've met. Also, he's one of the funniest. Since he was in town, I invited him to speak at our youth services. Perfect. I don't have to speak and I can relax a few days before the mayhem of camp.

Jeff arrived but he didn't come alone. He came with two other guys, one of whom I had met before and the other whom I'd never met. I got up to greet Jeff and after a brief hello he left me alone with the stranger. I was somewhat irritated that Jeff left me alone with this guy. I sat down and introduced myself.

"Hi, my name's Mike."

"I'm Ray," he replied.

"Okay . . . so what do you do, Ray?"

"I'm a pastor."

"Really? Where?"

"Waikele."

"Oh. What's the name of your church?"

"Hope Chapel Waikele."

"Come again?" I replied, somewhat dumbfounded.

"Hope Chapel Waikele," he said.

Now I was really irritated. Not only had Jeff brought these guys with him (which meant he and I were not likely to be hanging out after church), but he had joined the conspiracy of getting me to leave Hope Chapel Kane'ohe and forcing me to move to Hope Chapel Waikele, way on the other side of the island. The hot side. In retrospect, it felt somebody was trying to mess with my destiny, manipulating the situation behind the scenes of *my life*. Someone was pulling strings and calling shots that were designed to set me up and make me think this was all divine providence.

This was what I feared most. This was precisely what I did not want to happen. I wanted the pure call of God. I didn't want to do something that seemed strategic and convenient for everyone else. I didn't want to do something that looked very logical and worst of all, I didn't want to be "pushed upstairs."

When a great player is too old they make him an assistant coach. Or if a coach is falling behind the times and producing less winning seasons, in order to be gracious, management offers him a job in the front office instead, making room for the younger guy and saving his dignity. I didn't want to become a senior pastor yet. I knew it was inevitable but not yet. I didn't want Pastor Ralph or anyone else messing with my future.

When I met Ray, it was as if all my suspicions were being confirmed. My insecurities, along with my self-preservation instinct began working in the short moments of my dialogue with Ray Arney, the pastor sitting opposite me in the courtyard.

I leaned over and said, "You're leaving, aren't you?"

"How do you know? That's supposed to be confidential."

"Never mind how I know, I just know. Who brought you here? Who put you up to this?"

"Jeff brought me."

"Yeah, right. I'm sure Ralph told him to talk to you and bring you so you could convince me to take your place, making me think this is 'so God' to make it all happen this way." I have been known to get a little aggressive and this was one of those times.

Ray countered, "Nobody told me to come. Jeff doesn't know anything. We've just been good friends since the days we went to his old church here in Hawai'i." He looked very sincere, like he was telling me the truth. I became curious.

"You should take it. You'd be good," he continued.

"How do you know? You've never heard me preach."

"I just know. Besides, I've heard of you."

I thought to myself, *Yeah, right. Butter me up and go for the ego. Typical pastor.*

Then he said, "You have to hurry and make a decision because I'm leaving soon."

"If it's such a good church, why are you leaving?" I was not only daring him but also double-daring him.

"Because I've burned out. I've been bi-vocational for five years now and it's taken a toll. The church needs someone with fresh vision to take it to the next level. Hey, maybe you can stop by and preach this weekend or next."

"Burnout? I'm sorry to hear that. No, I wouldn't want to preach there. I think it's unethical, preaching at a church without them knowing I'm a candidate."

But Ray was persistent, and in retrospect, I'm glad he was. He ended by saying that I should at least stop by and visit the church the following weekend.

Hi Ho, Hi Ho, It's Off to Camp...

In the meantime, off to camp we went. It was an amazing camp. I wasn't sure if it would be my last. I prayed every morning, took walks by myself to ask the Lord for direction. I was hoping for a sign in the sky, perhaps some lightning, being so high up on the mountains of O'ahu. I was hoping I'd hear a voice from God, speaking out of the clouds saying, "You, Anointed One! Yes, you are my chosen vessel. Before the foundations of the earth were set, I set you apart to take this church and reach untold millions for My glory." Who could blame me?

I know my delusional thoughts of being The Anointed One seemed over the top. Truthfully, I was deathly afraid of leaving Hope Chapel Kane'ohe. I wasn't secure in my leadership ability or knowledge of the Word, and I felt absolutely unworthy. I'd wake up every day that week and go to a lookout with a cup of

Truthfully, I was deathly afraid of leaving Hope Chapel Kane'ohe.

coffee, sit on a big rock and just look out over the horizon with the ocean below me. There, I'd pray and look toward the community that was in question, asking if that was the place. I did that every day for six days.

As camp pastor, I thought about the students and how much I loved them. I didn't feel ready to move on. My heart was firmly entrenched in youth ministry. I recalled once having no desire to be a youth pastor. But all of that changed in a matter of months and I loved every minute of it. They were easy to speak to once they knew you loved and respected them. They would give it right back to me. Especially our leadership team. The student leaders were phenomenal and picked up quickly. Yet as each day went by, it seemed that a slow detachment was forming in my heart. It was as if I could see the countdown clock had begun. Funny, that this camp became one of the best camps ever!

It reminded me of the walk Jesus took with Peter and John in John 21. At the campfire Jesus asks Peter, "Do you love me more than these?" In retrospect, I was being asked the same question: "Mike, do you love me more than these?"

For me, "these" represented the students, the leadership opportunity, or even my own security. Then I recalled Matthew 6:33 (NKJV) when Jesus said, "But seek first the kingdom of God and His righteousness, and all these things shall be added to you." God was asking me to trust Him with a whole new set of "these" things; trusting in Him to exchange the old ones for some new ones.

LEAVE BEHIND WHAT GOT YOU HERE

Friend, whatever you are doing and whatever you're called to do, take an inventory of the "these things" you currently have and treasure and thank the Lord for them. Chances are you had to say goodbye to some old "these things" before the Lord beckoned and promoted you to a new level of "these things." And if you take the time to look back, I'm sure you'd find things that were difficult to part with because you loved them, became attached to them and even possibly found identity in them.

We always like to say, "Don't look back. Forge ahead, keep your determination." We must move ahead and say goodbye to the things that were once critical to our development. Then, from a safe distance away, often defined by time and miles, we can safely look back and say, "I'm so glad I let go of what was good at the time, in order to receive what was great in the future."

WHAT GOT YOU HERE WON'T TAKE YOU THERE

While on a trip to Israel, I was watching a National Geographic special on the Space Shuttle. It was fascinating watching how the shuttle exerts incredible amounts of fuel through two solid fuel rocket boosters. In the beginning stages of liftoff, the rocket boosters would explode with 7.8 million pounds of thrust to push the shuttle further and further away from the launch pad in order to get it into the atmosphere.[3]

During this stage, the shuttle is going through its most critical phase, liftoff. In this phase, immense pressure is being placed on the housing of the shuttle. All of the fuel contained in the boosters burns up at a rate of 4.5 tons per second. The purpose of the boosters is to launch the shuttle to its highest altitude.

But the rocket boosters, which were used to get the shuttle safely to orbit, would no longer be useful.[4]

What was once critical to the mission, would now have to be left behind, otherwise it would endanger the mission and hold back the shuttle from accomplishing its intended purpose: pioneering new frontiers. If the solid rocket boosters were not jettisoned, it is probable that the shuttle would be pulled back

❦

What got you here, won't take you there. God was about to show me the "there."

❦

to earth's atmosphere and plunge into the sea at tremendous loss of technology and, most of all, lives. This proves the widely held theory that what got you here, won't take you there. God was about to show me the "there."

Halfway through the camp, Lisa called my phone while I was taking an early morning walk before breakfast. "We just got a thank-you card from Doug and Karen Campbell. They thanked us for serving the Lord and gave us a gift certificate to a Waikiki hotel for three days and two nights!" The Campbells were a great family in our church. Karen was a great team player on Lisa's children's ministry team. Doug was the local Christian radio general manager at the time and a big encourager to Lisa and me. They also had a son who was an eleventh grade student leader in our youth group with a strong evangelistic gift. He was also one of the most fun kids ever to come through HCKB.

When Lisa called, I was so missing her by then, I couldn't wait until she and the girls came to the campsite. And when she called with the good news about a Waikiki getaway I couldn't help but get excited about being alone with the most beautiful woman in all of Hawai'i. The excitement soon dampened.

She said, "Isn't that great? Now we can go and fast and pray about this church." *Fast and pray?* The only kind of prayer that I was thinking about doing in Waikiki was praying a blessing over my food and saying my prayers before going to bed. "Prayer and fasting?" I said. "Nobody goes to Waikiki to fast and pray. Especially about a church. People go there to eat and enjoy one another's company, you know what I mean? Babe, it's been a long time since we've been together. . . ." But my Proverbs 31 woman would not be deterred. "This is the Lord giving us an opportunity for us to seek Him, Mike. We have to take this seriously. I'm feeling more and more like this might be His will for us." She was right.

This was God's way of giving us some uninterrupted time to seek His will. I was beginning to wonder if the Lord was once again orchestrating things like the "chance" meeting with Ray Arney at the church. Who could argue with Lisa's logic? Camp ended with a bang and I couldn't help but wonder if this could very well be my last time up on that mountain.

FASTING IN THE LAND OF PLENTY

Waikiki was all that it was cracked up to be. We spent a lot of time in prayer. We walked, talked, and prayed some more. What sticks out the most was the last day of our getaway. We packed our bags and prepared to go to the front desk to check out and head home. But before we left, Lisa and I really needed to be on the same page on this decision.

One thing I've learned through the years is to trust my wife's wisdom. I remember taking her hands in mine and asking her, "So, what do you think? What's the Lord saying to you?" Lisa replied, "I remember a while ago when you thought we were called to plant a church in Portland. You thought you were ready then but I knew in my heart that you weren't. I believe you answered a call to be a church planter someday but I didn't think it was the season and knew we needed more time with Ralph. But now it's different. Now, I look at you and you look like Moses when he had just come down from the mountain after spending time with the Lord—you have a glow about you. I believe you're ready and now is the time." Those words meant so much to me. Knowing Lisa was behind me would help me to do anything the Lord called us to do.

Still, I was struggling with something. I had heard that answering the call of God on your life was so much more exciting: Moses and the burning bush, David and the visit from the prophet Samuel, the huge luau thrown in his honor at the end of the anointing ceremony. All of these things went through my mind. I was hoping for some kind of "Bam!" from heaven, something more significant, more exciting, and with more pizzazz. That worried me. I was hoping for something that was more concrete, something that I could point to and say with 100 percent confidence that I was unequivocally, undeniably called by the Holy Spirit, like Abraham, to pack up and "leave my father's house and go to a country I will show you."

Yet something had happened in that week. My heart began to change. I went from an attitude of self-preservation (holding onto position) and self-interest (what was familiar and comfortable) to one of total surrender. I now only wanted to do what Jesus wanted me to do. And if that meant leaving what was familiar and what

I went from an attitude of self-preservation (holding onto position) and self-interest (what was familiar and comfortable) to one of total surrender.

I loved and following Jesus out of obedience then I knew that I would never lose. The bottom line was that if Jesus was calling me to go to Waikele, I was willing to go.

And that's what happened. My heart changed. I began thinking about the church and the possibilities. In retrospect, like Peter, Jesus was calling me out of the boat. It was definitely Jesus and He was calling me to leave the safety of the boat and step into the unfamiliar and the unknown.

I reflected on the prophetic words of Jean Darnall a year prior, and to the voice of the Lord in the car as I had driven to youth service. My chance encounter with Ray before camp was a critical element. I quickly added them up and deduced that this was indeed the Lord calling me to a new level of faith and obedience to answer His call. The proof for me was the change in my heart. I went from someone who had an immediate "no" for Pastor Ralph when it was first offered to me, to come to the place where I said, "God, I'll go wherever You want me to go, say what You want me to say, do what You want me to do and be whatever You want me to be."

After hearing Lisa's last words we decided to make a covenant before the Lord in that hotel. We took hold of each other's hands and prayed. We left that room with a commitment to leave HCKB and head for new territory.

In the Hawaiian language, *aloha* is widely used in several different scenarios. You'll be greeted by this word whether you are a tourist coming here on vacation or a college student returning home for the holidays. Its simple translation means *hello. Aloha* has two other meanings as well. For instance, it's used to express your love for someone. In Hawai'i, we are known as being the Aloha State and its people are said to exude the *aloha* spirit. It means we have great love for people, and it's true. But there is a translation of this word that is used, along with the other two definitions that have strong emotions tied to its usage. That third and final translation for *aloha* means *farewell* or *goodbye*. This is often used at airports in Hawai'i when we are speaking an emotional farewell or goodbye to someone we hold dear to our hearts. In this case, I would be saying *aloha* to a people (HCKB) and in a sense, to a calling I had treasured.

A Defining Moment

We always hear about defining moments. Often these moments are tied to an event and where you were and what you were doing at the time. For my parents, it was the assassination of President John F. Kennedy. For me, it was the explosion of the Space Shuttle Discovery on January 28, 1986. In that tragedy astronaut Ellison Onizuka perished, along with six others on that tragic day. I still remember watching it from my dorm room, stunned into silence. I mention this here because I had dreams of being an astronaut. Just months before, astronaut Onizuka spoke at an assembly at high school, leaving me inspired to follow through on one of my childhood dreams of being a fighter pilot. What I witnessed that day was that an average boy from Hawai'i, from a small town, could overcome the obstacles placed before him to become one of our nation's finest citizens. That was a defining moment for me.

Another generation would say September 11, 2001, has that distinction in their minds. Defining moments are often tied to tragedy. However, defining moments are also attached to things we commonly celebrate. A first kiss, a graduation ceremony, a wedding day, the birth of a child—we all have a few.

One interesting thing about defining moments is that you can remember them like it happened yesterday, and it seems the more you tell the story the more vivid it becomes. Or, in some cases, the more you keep adding to the "legend" of the moment. I was in the midst of one that would become more acute in the minutes ahead.

As Lisa and I drove home from Waikiki, I called Ralph in his office. "Hi, Ralph!"

"Mike, how was Waikiki?"

"Great!" I nervously replied not wanting to reveal too much excitement. I continued cautiously, "Ralph, we haven't had a chance to really get more than a few moments here or there to discuss the new church and I was wondering if I could come and talk to you at the office. Like, now. Is that okay with you?"

"Sure! Come on over."

I dropped Lisa off at home and headed to the office. I knocked on Ralph's door and was welcomed in. After taking our seats, I began asking two important questions that I needed answers to before I said "Yes" to accepting the pastorate of the church.

I sat down, took a deep breath, and exhaled. "Ralph, I need to know: Why wouldn't you want to send me to Honolulu? Why all the way out to Waikele?" (Waikele is about a thirty-minute drive from downtown Honolulu). The population of the island of O'ahu was about a million people at the time, with most of the people concentrated near the city of Honolulu. In fact, Honolulu has the highest concentration of people in the state, many of whom live in surrounding suburbs and in high-rise apartments and condos.

So my logic was to send me where the most people were. There were a couple of megachurches doing a great job reaching people within that vicinity, along with a couple of other churches in that area. I felt that if we planted a new church in urban Honolulu, as opposed to taking over a fifteen-year-old church in Waikele, we might be able to do the same and achieve similar results.

"I thought about that," he replied. "But I recall Pastor Jack Hayford moving out to the valley in Southern California and although the church was located farther away from downtown L.A., the growth came to them (Church on the Way in Van Nuys, California). Younger families, who couldn't afford to live closer to the city, began buying homes farther and farther away from the city and his church was able to serve those people of those growing suburbs. I see the same happening for you."

Although Waikele was already fully developed, the next few phases of home developments began moving westward, past Waikele and farther north as well. In fact, when I asked a realtor friend of mine for some demographics he told me that there were 150,000 people living within a three-mile radius of Waikele! The potential for a great harvest was huge.

"You know the students who were once in your ministry? One day they're going to get married and they'll move out to your end because that's the most likely place that they can afford. They'll start coming to your church and begin raising their families there." He was right—that's exactly what has happened. That took care of question number one.

The next question I would ask would be the toughest. I wasn't sure what kind of reaction I'd get, because I didn't want to disrespect Ralph, but I knew that if I was going to leave, I needed to have this settled in my heart. The next inhale

❧

With pain on his face and softness in his eyes, he said, "You are my son."

❧

was one with more physical manifestation. I actually shuddered. Finally, I said, "Are you trying to graciously get rid of me to make it a perceived win-win? Actually, I guess what I'm really trying to ask you, Ralph, is . . . are you trying to make room for your son, Carl?"

He looked at me and his face got red. I wasn't sure if I had upset him but I was sure about to get an answer. With pain on his face and softness in his eyes, he said, "You are my son." Wow. That was a heavy moment. A defining moment.

At that moment, I wanted to jump out of my chair and hug him and tell him, "Yes! Yes! I am your son and you are my father. You only want the best for me, don't you? Yes, you do! Thank you, thank you! Ralph! I will go. I will go anywhere you send me. I am like a son to you? I'll do anything. I'll wash your car. I'll move to Mongolia if you want me to. Why? Because I am your son, and you are my father, and in me you . . . are . . . well . . . pleased!" But of course, I didn't.

I don't fully recall what happened next, but I do know I was emotional. And I'll leave it at that. We composed ourselves and began planning my exit. I had two weeks before I would hold my first service and be anointed with oil, prayed for, and formally introduced to the church. We had no time to lose.

---

[1] http://archives.starbulletin.com/2003/09/28/special/story4.html

[2] Estimation from Malcolm Ching, President, Waikele Community Association

[3] Brian Dunbar, *Marshall's Role in Space Shuttle*, NASA,
    http://www.nasa.gove/centers/marshall/shuttle_station/shuttle.html (April 2011).

[4] June Malone, *Two Plus One Makes History*, NASA, http://www.nasa.gov/centers/marshall/news/news/releases/2005/05-024. html (March 2005).

CHAPTER 7

IT'S SMALLER THAN YOU THINK

Sizing Up Your Challenge with Fresh Perspective

"Therefore I do not run like someone running aimlessly;
I do not fight like a boxer beating the air."
1 Corinthians 9:26

Looking back, I would have to say the fear of failure was looming in my mind. I wanted the new church to grow larger than my youth ministry. I know that sounds bad, but I somehow knew there was an influential church in me (meaning, I believed God had equipped me to lead something greater).

I was coming from a church that oozed with vision. Under Ralph's leadership, my eyes had witnessed the possibilities of shepherding a large flock and reaching thousands for Christ. I'm not prideful when I say that I hoped and, dare I say, expected to lead even more people. At the same time, I feared not reaching my potential. What if they don't like me? What if I encounter people who are unwilling to be led by a young guy who isn't experienced as a senior pastor? What if the church doesn't grow? Yes, I understood it is Jesus who builds the Church, but it isn't as if I could hang out by the beach and come back and it would've grown!

It didn't take long to realize what was going to help me overcome all this non-sense—faith in God and in what He was calling Lisa and me to do. That faith needed to grow stronger and bigger than my fears. Still, I needed to reconcile in my heart if I could pastor a church of less than a hundred people for the rest of my life. It took some quick soul-searching, and in the end I resolved to God and myself, "Yes, I can and will if that's what the future holds."

IT IS WHAT IT IS

Pastors who are faithful to their flocks, all around the world, are my heroes. I never judge a pastor by the size of his church. Why? Because I don't appreciate being judged myself. Imagine if a pecking order is immediately established just because one pastor has a larger church than the next pastor. As we well know, the pound for pound principle is a reminder that it's not the size of a church or business (or boxer) that matters. It is whether you are making a difference with what you've been given.

Not everyone has been given the tools others have. Not everyone is afforded the same opportunities that some have been graced with. Not all are able to go to seminary or Bible college or given *this* thing or fought through *that* thing or the *other* thing. Again, the servants in Jesus' parable were given talents "according to what he was capable of." So our "talents" will never be equal.

You can't change your starting point. As a kid, did you ever wish your parents were rich? Okay, maybe I'm the only one. The point I'm making is that just as no one can change who their biological parents are, you can't change how much talent you've been given from the start. What you get is what you've got,

You can't change your starting point.

whether one, two, or five talents. But, like the parable, every one of us, pastor or not, will be rewarded and disciplined for what we do with what we are given, regardless of what it is. It is what it is.

I have already talked about numbers in ministry. They don't reflect everything, but they are a pretty good measurement of growth. Of course, other factors can be viewed as growth, such as the spiritual growth of the congregation. We examine the "condition of our flocks" based on their knowledge of the Bible and on their prayer life. We also measure their relational maturity, their ability to get along with one another. For me, a big indicator of spiritual growth is how they are doing in witnessing to non-believers, whether they continue to take His Commission seriously: "Go and make disciples!"

One of my pet peeves about some Christians who describe themselves as mature in the Lord is they think evangelism is the job of the pastor on Sunday morning, or that evangelism has to be someone's spiritual gift. Or they say, "I was once like you, Sonny Boy, but now that I've matured and cooled down I leave that to the younger Christians." That's a faulty perception.

The truth of the matter is a mature believer in Jesus Christ is doing "all of the above." They're in the Word, they're discipling other believers, they're in prayer, they're sharing their faith, and they're leading or at least attempting to lead others to Jesus. So yes, growth is not only measured by numbers but by the overall health of a ministry or organization. So if a church is healthy, there should be growth.

MEDIOCRITY IS NEVER THE GOAL

When people think about venturing out on their own, they don't stand boldly with their hands on their hips like a superhero and declare, "When I get my chance and God gives me a shot, I will strive to become . . . (drum roll, please) *mediocre!* Yes, that's it! Mediocrity is the goal!" No one goes back to college after ten years removed from school, believing in their heart they will be terrible at what they aspire to do. Or when someone starts a family, who would plan to raise rebellious children or cheat on their spouse? Failure, let alone mediocrity, is never the goal.

So let's eliminate failure from this discussion. We should, however, address "mediocrity" for a moment. Webster's defines *mediocre* as an adjective: "Of moderate or low quality, value, ability, or performance: ordinary, so-so."

Who wants to be described as mediocre? It gives off the air of someone who is the opposite of faithful. However, mediocre could be used to describe the person in the parable who buried the talent. The reason why we won't describe this person as anything less than mediocre is because he was given *something*. He didn't receive two or five talents like the other servants, but he wasn't passed by altogether. He was given something. Even so, let me take creative license for a moment and look at the result of burying the talent. It is safe to say the man who received one talent had mediocre results *because of his actions*, which were unlike the actions of the other two.

But why would someone do that? Why would someone bury what he's been given when the instructions of the master were quite clear? It's possible he thought to himself, *One talent? Really? If that's what you think I'm capable of then what's the use in trying? I'll give you the results you probably expect of me.* He could have attached his self-worth to the amount of talent he was given.

We also see some fear and misperceptions of the master's wishes. I've faced this on several occasions. I've had leaders basically tell me, "I wasn't clear about your instructions, so I did nothing." They didn't ask me for clarification yet they blamed me for their lack of faithfulness! My response? Something along the lines of, "With that attitude and perception, around here your place on the team is an NFL." No, not the National Football League but "Not For Long."

Like the man with one talent, these are usually diversionary tactics and lame excuses. But what was the man in the parable thinking? I have an idea: He was content to be average. Average describes something or someone that is *typical, common* or *ordinary*. And here is where the problem lies.

VISION

There is a shortage of one of the most important and crucial commodities in the world today: vision. One reason we lack vision is that we sometimes succumb to being average and then we are content with average results.

My personal opinion is that most of us start out with great hopes and high aspirations to do something of significance. But when our best-laid plans do not materialize as envisioned, we shrink back and dumb down our vision to the size of our circumstances. For example, you may not be where you expected to be in this stage of your life or ministry, so due to discouragement, you might be afraid to *dream of what could be.* Your marriage may not be what you want it to

There is a shortage of one of the most important and crucial commodities in the world today: vision.

be, and after years of trying to change one another, the temptation is to give up and settle for less in the marriage—mediocrity.

Perhaps even more tragic is that I have seen others who started out desiring to be extraordinary in their pursuits, and for whatever reason, began to convince themselves that they were *called to be average.* We will sometimes use tired expressions to comfort ourselves: "Oh, I guess it's not meant to be," or "I'm not supergifted so that must not be for me." I've heard it said that many pastors have less confidence today than when they first started off—they felt more confident in their ability to lead a church in their first two years than in year eight, nine and ten. I'll explain more about this in a moment, but for now, friend, do not believe for a minute you are called to be average in anything you do. You are a child of the King. The Lord has given you an inheritance. You have been called to be extraordinary! Not just ordinary. The pound for pound principle is all about being *the best you can be* in your weight-class, becoming the best you can be no matter where you are or what you do.

SOURCES OF MEDIOCRITY

Let us expose two sources of mediocrity: The first is culture, the other is conformity. Now, in many circles, conforming to something is viewed as a good thing. On the other hand, the Holy Spirit commands us through Paul the apostle: "Do not conform to the pattern of this world, but be transformed by the renewing of your mind. Then you will be able to test and approve what God's will is—his good, pleasing and perfect will" (Romans 12:2). But the definition I want to run with in terms of conformity has to do with someone who blends into the background of uniformity.

In Japan, a country I love and whose people are some of the most kind, there is an axiom in the psyche of the culture that seems to keep many people mired in mediocrity. The saying goes something like, "The nail that stands out gets pounded down." Can you imagine how this idea affects people who want to rise above the routine? However, if you ride the trains of Japan or go to places where young people hang out, you'll see some people who definitely stand out from the crowd. They dress with flair, apparently okay with being a nail that stands out. It could be chalked up to rebellious youthfulness, but whatever you call it, it's not conformist behavior.

For years, people have said it is impossible to build a growing and prevailing church in Japan. It's not true. Pastors Rod and Vivian Plummer moved to Japan less than a decade ago to prove otherwise. They were told all the statistics of failed church plants in a nation that was referred to as a "graveyard for missionaries." Against all odds and those "well-intentioned" opinions, they now pastor one of Japan's most vibrant, influential, and reproductive churches. They

For years, people have said it is impossible to build a growing and prevailing church in Japan. It's not true.

exceed 1,500 in attendance and the average age of their congregation is twenty-five! Rod once told me they just decided they would not receive the pessimistic reports, and they were naïve enough to pull it off! They refused to conform and instead decided to transform the city of Tokyo.

When I was young, I struggled with conformity that stifled me for a few years. Something happened when I was eleven and still sticks with me. The University of Hawai'i at Hilo Vulcans won the '77-'78 NAIA Basketball Championship and our elementary school hosted two stars from that team, Jay "The Bird" Bartholomew and Bill O'Rear. The huge hoops fan I was, Bill

O'Rear was a favorite of mine because he was small and could handle the ball like Houdini could handle a deck of cards. At one point during the assembly, Bill asked for two volunteers from the crowd. Friends "volunteered" me and another boy in my class, Waldo. Although Waldo was bigger than me (as were most boys in my class), I was one of the better basketball kids with "handles." Waldo was far more popular than me and the girls really liked him. He was smooth.

So Bill called us up and the kids cheered. I was a little shy but proud to represent my friends' hopes and dreams. Bill showed us a ball-handling drill that had us facing one another, bent over at a slight angle, with hands behind our back. He explained that when he dropped the ball we were to wait for the third bounce of the ball, and then we were free to reach out and grab the ball. The first kid to grab the ball would be the winner, and the one who was able to grab the ball two times out of three attempts would be declared the champion of the universe, um, elementary school.

Due to my strong resemblance to Flash Gordon, my fast twitch muscles in my forearms and shoulders, and the quickness of my hands, I won the first round. Waldo countered and won the second round. The suspense began to rise. Every third- through sixth-grader who had any understanding knew that the gravity of playground politics and supremacy hung in the balance. But as quickly as you could say "flip-flop crowd," the assembly seemed to sway away from my favor to my opponent. They began chanting, "Waldo! Waldo! Waldo!" and to my dismay whatever voices supporting me were soon drowned out by the fickle crowd. Or perhaps they went turncoat on me. It was at that moment I began to rationalize away my reason for giving my all and winning.

In all seriousness, I began thinking to myself, *I am not supposed to win, expected to win, nor do I want to win.* I made a decision based upon conformity and I intentionally gave away the third and final round. As soon as it was over, I stood midcourt and congratulated Waldo (who today is still a good friend of mine), while acting like that was how it was supposed to be. Pity.

Why did I do this? In retrospect, it seemed as though it would have been best for everyone involved if I played things out the way everyone expected. I conformed. Okay, I know this is sixth-grade stuff but don't we still do this at times? Do we sell ourselves short because we are afraid of sticking out? Do we decide it's best that we just *blend in and conform* to what we're expected to be? If I continued to have this kind of faulty thinking as an adult, our church would likely not be in the position we are in today. This type of conformity is the kind that keeps us thinking and dreaming small. It holds us back from becoming all God wants us to be.

Hawaiian culture is a bit like Japan's and perhaps others. We tend to want to blend in with others so we don't stick out. Perhaps it happens in your context as well. There is something in our psyche that tells us we don't deserve to succeed. When this happens, we are prone to shrink back and "dumb down" the size of our dreams and goals. If you believe you don't have the right to succeed, why should anyone else, right? That's why prevailing through your circumstance and breaking away from the pack brings criticism—but it brings freedom as well.

I'm the kid who broke several of his gifts on Christmas Day because I wanted to take my toys apart to see their inner workings. I had no idea how to put them back together! But I enjoyed the freedom of trying to figure out how they operated. I carried this interest into adulthood.

For example, while on staff at HCKB, if I didn't understand a decision or agree with it, I didn't shy away from asking about it. Near the end of my time there, we were reorganizing the structure of the staff and church. I respectfully asked why it was being done a certain way and voiced another option. It wasn't

I always wanted to understand the "why" of a decision so I could fully support the "how."

the direction the senior staff was interested in taking, and I understood that. In that instance and a few others, I could tell some of my peers were irritated with me. Sometimes I would spot a few of them rolling their eyes, probably thinking, *There he goes again.*

It's not easy to stand out and ask tough questions. My pushback never reached a rebellious level, but I always wanted to understand the "why" of a decision so I could fully support the "how." Of course, I understood biblical authority, and if push came to shove, even if I didn't understand the why, I was able to carry out the vision and the strategy of the leadership. Sure, there were times I might not have agreed with a decision (not that it would have mattered), but at least I knew the reasoning behind it and could take "ownership" of leaders' plans. Had I succumbed to peer pressure and conformed in a less than healthy way, I'm not sure how things would have turned out for Lisa and me. It pays to ask questions.

CHAPTER 8

THE CULTURE OF CONTENDERS

Created by Default or Design?

"Everywhere we go,
people breathe in the exquisite fragrance.
Because of Christ, we give off a sweet scent rising to God,
which is recognized by those on the way
of salvation—an aroma redolent with life."
2 Corinthians 2:15–16 The Message

People come from all over the world to Hawai'i to experience the surf, the beaches, and simply take in all the wonder of God's creation. I must say, of all the beautiful places in the world, it seems like God has placed His special favor in the middle of the Pacific Ocean. It's as though He said on the day of creation, "Want to see something amazing? Watch this!" And voila! Hawai'i!

If you haven't visited Hawai'i, I hope you've been able to talk to someone who has vacationed here. They surely told you about the white sandy beaches and maybe the crystal-blue surf of the North Shore, the lush vegetation of Kaua'i, or the volcanoes of the Big Island. But I'm guessing they also eventually talked about the people of Hawai'i. Our island culture makes a big impact, and it is the people who perpetuate Hawaiian culture.

If I were to tell you about the wonderful Hawaiian culture, I would start with the Hawaiian language and its critical role in perpetuating the culture. Take away the *'olelo*, or the language of the indigenous people, and Hawaiian culture would disappear.

Hawaiian culture is characterized by several key words. For example, regardless if you are an ethnic or an Asian who grew up in Hawai'i, Hawaiian culture is one of *'ohana*, or family. Whether of Hawaiian ethnicity or not, we believe in the strong value of *'ohana*. Also, the word *hanai* (adoption) refers to the common practice of Hawaiians to welcome someone who is not blood-related into

Whether of Hawaiian ethnicity or not, we believe in the strong value of *'ohana*.

their family. Doesn't all this make you just want to get on a plane and experience the culture of our islands?

Because I came from an identifiable culture of church at Hope Chapel Kane'ohe Bay, I knew what kind of culture we wanted at Hope Chapel West O'ahu. Likewise, we knew what kind of culture we didn't want.

Before we proceed further on the subject, allow me to define culture the way I see it in the context of a church or organization: *Culture is the underlying, overarching environment of an organization that shapes its mores and values, which in turn determines its success.* The culture, the atmosphere, or the environment of an organization, whether a business or a church, will heavily influence the organization's level of success (or fruitfulness). This could be applied to a family, a sports team, to almost anything involving groups of people.

When I think of great sports teams, what immediately comes to mind is the Green Bay Packers of the 1960s and 1970s. Their coach, Vince Lombardi, has been venerated as one of the great sages of sports leadership. Or we could examine the Boston Celtics of the 1950s and 1960s and talk about the mystique of the Boston Garden (or Gah-den, if you're from New England) and its parquet floor and "leprechauns" that make up their culture. In creating a winning culture, Celtics coach Red Auerbach demanded that the older players on the team mentor the younger players, creating a culture of mentorship that translated into eight titles from 1959 to 1966. We could look at John Wooden who coached the UCLA Bruins men's basketball teams that won ten NCAA titles, including seven straight from 1967 to 1973. Wooden has been quoted as saying that he never had to yell in a game because he did all of his preparation and yelling in practice. If the team practiced well, they'd play well.

The first thing to notice about these teams is that they all had a culture of "winning." They expected to win. How? Well, they had great talent. But you can have all the talented and gifted people in the world, but if they aren't work-

You either create the kind of culture you want, or, by default, a culture will be created for you.

ing together, it all goes to waste. Legendary baseball coach Casey Stengel once said, "It's easy to get good players. It's getting them to play together that's the hard part!" The Packers, Celtics and Bruins were all able to do that.

In all of these examples of winning teams, the largest contributing factor to the success of these teams would unquestionably be their coaches. I believe that each one of the legendary coaches mentioned above took personal responsibility for the culture created on their teams. A team with a healthy culture that is stated clearly and pursued diligently is very likely to win their share of games (and even titles).

CREATE THE CULTURE, OR IT WILL BE CREATED FOR YOU

It is my opinion that you either create the kind of culture you want, or, by default, a culture will be created for you. If you do not intentionally create the culture of your team, the players will haphazardly create it. If you abdicate this essential duty as the leader of a ministry, you forfeit one of your most powerful leadership tools. However, if you intentionally set a healthy culture, your team will thrive. This dynamic works in families too. As parents, you can determine the kind of culture your family will have. But if you don't take initiative, your children will end up creating the culture by default. Whatever your sphere of leadership, either you create the culture or it will be created for you. And when someone else shapes the culture, what you get may not be what you want.

So, what kind of culture do *you* have? Do you like what you see, or are you irritated by how things are? If you don't like what's happening, take responsibility for what kind of culture is present and begin the process of becoming a "cultural architect." The obvious person to assume this role would be the leader of any church, business, or organization.

However, culture can also be shaped from those who are not at the top of the structure. For example, those on our team who have joined us through the years learn the culture of HCWO. The culture is articulated to them and they absorb it the longer they're with us. Culture is both caught and taught. We don't expect them to figure it out all on their own. That would be unfair to them and a mistake for us. We teach it. Then, they can *observe the culture* in action. Once they see and understand what our culture is, they are expected to contribute to the culture of our church and staff, and become *keepers of the culture*—guarding and protecting what is dear to our hearts. They are now equipped to understand it and empowered to share it.

IDENTIFY CULTURE PROBLEMS

The first thing you must do in order to shape the culture is to identify what exists.

It's likely you've walked into an office or into your home and felt some tension just by little cues you picked up. Maybe everyone seemed on edge. You were able to feel it. If it's an ongoing thing, chances are that tension has made its way into the culture of the office and has been there for a while. You may shy away from confronting it at first, but you have to be honest with yourself and let others be honest with you. You have to call it like it is. If it's unhealthy, call it that. If there are things about the culture you don't like, make that clear. As in almost anything, the first step to healing, freedom, or wholeness is to be able to admit what's wrong and then say, "This has got to change."

I remember one night while I was pastoring youth, a couple of women in their twenties visited our ministry. They were from Youth With A Mission based on the island of Maui, but visiting O'ahu for a few weeks. They appeared to be solid in their faith and I found out that one of them had the gift of prophecy. At the time, I wasn't very familiar with that particular spiritual gift but wanted to "experiment" with letting the Holy Spirit lead in that fashion.

So, in my desire to venture into an important yet relatively unknown area to me, I made a rookie mistake. I gave the prophecy-girl the opportunity to address the students with "whatever the Lord has placed on your heart." She got up and with great charisma and confidence said, "Hmmm. What is the Lord saying? Okay. The Lord is showing me there is a lack of unity in this ministry . . . *yadda, yadda, yadda, blah, blah, blah.*" I'm sure you can imagine what I was thinking as those words tumbled out of her mouth. *No, that's not what I was expecting! Oh, my. You couldn't be more wrong! Who is this girl and who invited her anyway? And who let her speak? Oh yeah. Me. You're an idiot, Michael Kai, for letting her up there!*

After I calmed down a few days later, I realized she was right. I hated to admit it. Now, whether that was prophetic or not, I'm not sure. I can tell you by experience that if you come from the outside and are quickly placed in a culture of disunity, you don't have to be prophetic to discern a problem in the atmosphere. Like a fish out of water, you can quickly sense something is different once you enter into a new environment. In this case, it took someone from the outside to tell me there was something wrong with our culture. I was in it and it had become familiar and normal to me. So, step one, *identify culture problems.*

Own Up To Culture Problems

After you identify the culture problem, the second thing to do to shape culture is to *own up to it.* That's what was so hard for me to do when it was brought to my attention. I was in denial for a few days. But as I prayed on it and pondered it, I realized I needed to make some changes. I've been told that denial is best kept as a river in Egypt (get it? De-Nile). Sometimes the hardest thing to do is to admit you have a problem.

It's like the story I once heard about a farmer who had a bloodhound dog wailing on his porch. His neighbor, a few acres away, came over on his tractor because he was wondering why in the world this bloodhound was wailing so loud for so long. So he gets to the house, walks up the stairs to the porch, looks at the dog and says, "Why's your bloodhound wailing, Billy Bob?" The old farmer looks at his neighbor from his rocking chair, takes his cob pipe from his teeth, and says, "He done got a nail that he's sittin' on right there, Jimmy Joe. Yes, sir, he's in a bit

Sometimes the hardest thing to do is to admit you have a problem.

of pain, that ol' bloodhound is." Jimmy Joe replied, "Well, ain't you gonna do sumpin' 'bout it?" Billy Bob replied, "Well, I reckon that when he finally admits he got a problem and he done get off the nail, I can help him. But until he admits that it hurt enough, I can't do nothin' for him. Guess it don't hurt enough!"

The moral of the story is, "Admit you have a problem!"

I'm sure you're not like that ol' bloodhound. But after you've *identified a culture problem*, after you've *owned up to it*, it's time for the third step: *deal with it.*

DEAL WITH IT

This problem with our youth ministries culture begged to be addressed. I knew the diagnosis; now I needed to follow through on a prescription. Otherwise, if left untreated, it would have slowly eaten away at the entire student ministry. The students had the most to lose if we did not change. It would be tragic to do what the man did in James 1:23–24: he looked in the mirror, turned around, walked away and forgot what he looked like and *did nothing about it*. So again, it's not enough to know what the problem is. You have to have courage to fight it and change the negative characteristics of your culture. I never could have fully understood culture and climates of a ministry back then because of my lack of experience, but I certainly understand it today. It took a while to turn it around, but we eventually prevailed in time to see some healthy results.

In my eleven years as a senior pastor, I have had three distinct occurrences in dealing with the effect of disunity creeping into our culture. Before I get into some level of detail, let me first say that I had to learn how to confront people as well as how to push for confrontation in order to come to a peaceful resolution. I firmly believe that if your destination for your family, workplace, or ministry is *peace*, it must go through a toll bridge called *conflict*. Because, *there will be a price to pay for peace*. We all want peace but we sometimes want *peace at all costs*. And when we do, we tolerate things we shouldn't be tolerating all in the name of peace. Avoiding the issue begins to enable those who are directly

If your destination for your family, workplace, or ministry is *peace*, it must go through a toll bridge called *conflict*.

involved and confuses those who are on the periphery. I needed to address this immediately. Confrontation and initiating conflict is a skill I developed over the years, but I will often initiate conflict to have peace.

Each case of disunity always involved a specific person as its root source. I could easily identify the results (fruit), but I had to dig deeper and in time would find the source (root) of the problem. And in all three cases, as usual, they involved someone very close to me in regards to a working relationship.

In one of those cases I wondered why we seemed to be barely cruising along on a "high seas yacht" built for speed. I couldn't put my finger on it, but our ministry wasn't going as fast as we expected. The winds were favorable and our sails were wide open. We were working hard, reaching a lot of people for Jesus. We had a level of momentum and were also about to move into our new facility, but everything seemed as slow as molasses.

But then the Holy Spirit revealed through some very unique and painful cir-cumstances (which I don't want to divulge at this writing) what the problem was and who was at its root. After this revelation came to light, the best way I can describe it was I realized our "yacht" was dragging its anchor all along. Everything looked great above the surface. All systems were a go or appeared that way. There were smiling faces on deck. But the anchor, a staff member, was dug in. After the initial hurt and shock, I pushed to reveal the conflict in order for us to have peace. As I previously stated, peace comes at a cost, but tem-porary hurt was needed for long-term healing. Everyone paid a price. The people he was leading had the pain of saying *aloha* to this person. There would be financial hardship on this person's family because of his actions. I paid a big price, too, in anxiety, in a partially ruined vacation (I couldn't stop thinking about it), but most of all it hurt me because I didn't see it coming. At my core, I'm a shepherd and I love people and want to be loved back. We achieved peace, but the conflict was costly. Not surprisingly, though, when we cut the anchor loose, we flew across the surface of the ocean.

Many of us don't like confrontation and as a result we don't have the peace we desire. Leaders who don't want to (or are unsure how to) confront a prob-lem situation or person for fear of the fallout will sometimes allow things to go unchecked and then it begins to spread. That's what happened to us in the above scenario. It spread to other staff members and leaders. I'm so glad we addressed it because we got it in time and removed the blinders from those who themselves were unable or unwilling to stand up to this person. Because many haven't been trained in healthy confrontation, we can overcompensate and become too strong and border on abuse. If you're a pastor or in management, it's so important to get that skill or find someone on your team who has the authority and respect to do that. You cannot afford to tolerate disunity. Hopefully, when a difficult person is confronted, he will repent and change, but if not, he's got to go. Show disunity the door.

That's why, when it comes to culture, whatever you tolerate soon becomes the "new normal." It becomes familiar. Like the story of the frog in the kettle, you'll soon boil over and not even notice because you did not feel the slight changes and increases in temperature. In the end, you'll wonder why someone is saying, "You're right! Frog really does taste like chicken."

One more thing I've learned is that you can confront things or people when it is still healthy. If you do it early enough, there can be win-win situations and it is very possible to achieve the desired outcomes you seek. We've even been able to coach our daughters on how to use healthy confrontation, following Jesus' principles in Matthew 18:15 to improve their friendships and even how to speak to their coaches and teachers.

MAKING THE CHANGE

If you want to change your culture, start by determining specifically what the source of the aggravation is. It could be a policy or procedure that keeps tripping up your effectiveness. Or, worse, it could be a person like I mentioned above. Whatever or whomever it is, it must be evaluated. Some people find it difficult to make the changes required once they discover the source (person). It is comparable to people who go to the doctor and leave with news that they have diabetes. After learning of the diagnosis, they never return for another

To make the change, sometimes you have to bid *aloha* to someone.

check up and fail to follow through on picking up their medication and changing their diet. Untreated, they face the possibility of losing their eyesight, possible amputation, and even death. The obvious lesson? Make the change. Sometimes you have to bid *aloha* to someone.

After removing specific aggravators, make it clear what you don't want your culture to be like and eliminate anything that doesn't line up with your conviction. You have to be resolute in your conviction and say, "That will not be a part of who we are," and make the necessary changes. I'm sure some of the changes will be difficult to implement because they may involve releasing people who are not willing to buy in to a new culture or improve the existing one. It will be hard, but it will be worth it. After you've done the tough work of eliminating, then *reinstate* the things you *do want*. Protect and guard your culture. With careful diligence and follow-through, you and your organization will begin to *elevate!* This is where you begin creating your "new normal."

CREATING WHAT YOU WANT

As I've said, either you create the culture or the culture will be created for you. Without an intentional approach from leadership about the culture, it will settle to the lowest level. Make no mistake about it. You must be intentional about the kind of culture you want to have.

But what if you have difficulty articulating the kind of culture you want? One of the best places to start is to *articulate what you don't want*. That's easy to do. What do you not want your church or organization to be like? What have you seen in another setting that makes you think, *Uh, we definitely don't want that happening here.* Call it like you see it.

After you've come up with a list of what you don't want, begin listing what you do want. Close your eyes, and answer this phrase: *the church I envision is* —————. Simple. I wish I'd started out with a clearly defined and expressed

Once a team is unified in a healthy culture, they will naturally produce victories.

culture from day one. I had it in my mind and in my heart, but to have it documented would have been very helpful for everyone else. So please don't just read past this and make a note to work on it someday—start writing your culture statement now.

Behind every great team is an esprit de corps, or a morale, to that team. Behind that morale is a culture, one that should be articulated, expressed, and taught. Combine all these elements and you'll find that a healthy culture will be *caught* by your team. Once a team is unified in a healthy culture, they will naturally produce victories—and there's no limit to what God can do with a church like that.

CHAPTER 9

YOU GET WHAT YOU GET

Defining Your Present Reality

"... to accept their lot and be happy in their toil—this is a gift of God."
Ecclesiastes 5:19

My daughters, Courtney, Rebekah, and Charis, have a nine-year gap between each of them, presenting definite pros and cons. One disadvantage is that the oldest doesn't get to grow up with the youngest. Also, Lisa and I will essentially be raising children in our home for a long, long time. I know some of you are thinking, *What? It's a joy and privilege.* I know, relax. In all seriousness, we have been blessed beyond measure with our girls and I thank God for each one of them and their uniqueness.

A few months ago our youngest, Charis (pronounced Ka-riss, which means *grace* in Greek), bought Rebekah a birthday gift out of her own savings. Pretty impressive for a five-year-old. But in an out-of-character moment, Bekah failed to show appreciation for the gift at the level that Charis had hoped for. Hurt, Charis ran to Lisa, crying, "She doesn't like my gift. Bekah is so mean, Mommy!" Needless to say, Bekah tried her best to comfort Charis, but our little stick of dynamite wasn't giving in so easily. Charis turned from Lisa's arms, spun around, and uttered a phrase that reminds me of the parable of the talents. With a defiant stance, a tear-stained face, and great emotion to complement her posture, my little five-year-old stated, "Bekah! You get what you get!"

So true, isn't it?

OUT THE DOOR

The time arrived to notify HCKB that I was leaving. We needed to make the announcement fast because we needed to get to Waikele within a couple of weekends. The denomination felt the public introduction must be made as soon as possible, so there was no time to waste. In fact, this wasn't a church plant so it wasn't treated as such. This would be more like a re-plant, so the strategy would have to be much different than if we were pioneering. Normally, Ralph would give us a year to hold interest-gathering meetings, build our core team, and launch with a bang both in resources and people. This was not one of those situations. We had a week. I was a little worried about the timing, but looking back, that's all we really needed. The ones the Lord called would be those who came. And as Charis would say, "You get what you get!"

That weekend Ralph announced to the church I was leaving for Waikele. He brought me up on the platform and commissioned me. To be honest, I expected to feel a lot more emotion, but Lisa was still going to be working at HCKB, and Rebekah and Courtney would also be there for a little while longer.

After the last service, we held a meeting to see who was interested in moving over to the new church with me. I held my breath. About forty people showed

I would have counted cockroaches if they had showed up.

up. That was all we needed. But those forty who would come with us were precious. In fact, I remember counting all forty myself. It didn't matter to me that we had twenty adults and twenty kids. Each person counted in my book, and I would have counted cockroaches if they had showed up. In fact, if a pregnant woman came with us, I would have counted her as three people because she might have been pregnant with twins.

At the new church in Waikele, there was an all-church meeting on a week-night prior to the "anointing" service. About twenty or so people attended. To me they all seemed to be sitting with their arms crossed with looks on their faces that said, "Oh, yeah? We'll just wait and see how this young, cocky kid is going to lead us." In reality, some did seem excited about me coming to Waikele because of my pedigree, having worked under Pastor Ralph. A few had met me in my multi-level marketing days. But there were enough in the crowd who were skeptical and voiced their concerns. "How long are you going to be here?" demanded one lady. *Longer than you*, I thought to myself. "I don't want to be treated like a number," said another. From the beginning, I faced a level of opposition.

PERSPECTIVES

Later, with my mouth agape and eyes wide-opened, I looked across the table at the divisional superintendent who was overseeing the transfer. We examined the church finances, ledger, membership log, and bylaws. In addition to the small amount in the checking account for monthly operational costs, there was $15,000 in savings. That was a lot of money, almost three times the amount I was used to handling in my youth checking account. Looking back, it wasn't much to finance a church with, but in my eyes, it was a fortune. I saw it as *seed to be planted*. And I had plans for how I was going to plant it. I was naïve, and in hindsight I'm glad that I was because I had no mental barriers for what to do with the money. I pondered the amount, which seemed like a gift to me. I saw it as an opportunity to gamble–er, plant seed.

I still couldn't believe $15,000 was just sitting in the savings account, unused, tucked away for safekeeping. It seemed like a waste earning less than 2 percent interest when it could be used for greater purposes. I guess fresh eyes and a "greenness" made me see things differently. Instead of seeing things as, "I need to save this for a rainy day or for something down the road," I saw things as,

"Wow! Here's our chance to take this amount and parlay it into something great!" I love the quote from C.T. Studd who said, "The gamblers for gold are so many, but the gamblers for God so few. Where are the gamblers for God?" I

When it comes to laying it all on the line for God, we hesitate. Why is that?

don't go to Las Vegas, but isn't that true? We find it so easy to place a bet on the table and accept the odds of losing hard-earned money. But when it comes to laying it all on the line for God, we hesitate. Why is that?

My plans for the money may not have been grandiose, but I used it to purchase advertising and laptops. We secured a spot on the local Christian radio station that went on at various times during the day right after Ralph's radio broadcast. Through Hope Chapel's name and Ralph's influence, the radio ad brought awareness to the Christian community that a Hope Chapel was in West O'ahu. Additionally, we advertised on the state's most listened-to secular radio station, as well as with the local newspaper, phone book, and through a new website and lots of eye-catching signage. Coupled with the laptops, most of the money was invested as *seed*.

Keep in mind that we didn't do these things thinking it was a magic bullet that would reach thousands for Jesus and then we could just wait for people to come pouring in. The core team that came with us, mixed with the present leadership that eventually warmed to us, didn't just sit around twiddling our thumbs in anticipation. We went to work. We went door-to-door on prayer walks in the community. We hung door-hangers with our church's advertisement on it, while praying. We served at the school and the neighboring towns. This would eventually bear fruit. The soil needed tilling and we needed to keep the pests away. We needed to water what we currently had along with what we had just planted. We fertilized it, trying to maintain the right environment. All this to say that our fresh perspective enabled us to see things and do things from a new angle that might not have been previously attempted.

THINK YOURSELF CLEAR

There is so much power in the way we see things. While one person can look at a situation and see one thing, another person coming in from the outside often sees something totally different. It is important to have a fresh perspective. You need to "think yourself clear."

You may be a pastor, a business owner, a leader of an organization, or a leader of your family. When you are in a season where you are the one, and there is no one else appearing on the horizon, a lot depends on you and how you respond. Then you've got to get some time away with the Lord. You must pray for a clear mind and a fresh perspective to see things as you've never seen them before. There will be the opinions of others and you'll be tempted to take a poll to see what others are saying. In the end, what it will come down to is, what is the Lord saying to you?

WHAT YOU HAVE IS ALL HE NEEDS

The way we view things can be the difference between a poverty mentality and having more than you need. A poverty mentality is characterized by feelings of scarcity and an attitude that reflects a stingy heart. This outlook can be detrimental to any endeavor. One of my favorite passages in the Old Testament is the story of Elisha and the widow (2 Kings 4:1–7). In a time of drought and

A poverty mentality is characterized by feelings of scarcity and an attitude that reflects a stingy heart.

famine in Israel, Elisha, a prophet of Israel, visits a widow. The nameless widow came crying to the man of God for answers and relief. With grief written all over her face she fell at his feet saying, "My husband has died and I have nothing in the house to feed my two young sons." Keep in mind the Bible gives us no other emotional clues or additional verbal exchange between them. However, I would imagine that after speaking comfort and showing genuine concern for the widow, he looked at her and spoke in a soothing voice, "Tell me, what do you have left in the house? Do you have *anything left* in the pantry?" She didn't have to think twice because for the last few weeks she had taken inventory of exactly what was left. When you haven't got much left, you end up staring in the cupboards for what doesn't exist.

We, like the widow, might be desperate and feel defeated in our own circumstances. Perhaps you've found yourself staring at the checkbook, asking yourself how you will pay the mortgage or the electricity and how many days until it all runs dry. Several minutes have gone by, but nothing changes on the ink and paper and the numbers continue to show you are headed for the negative. Or maybe you're staring out of the window, wondering when your wayward son or daughter is going to return home. Or you may have been gazing in the mirror, wondering where all the years have gone and how in the world you and your spouse drifted so far apart.

I can understand if you've quit trying because everywhere you turn can be a constant reminder of what you lack. You could almost ignore the checkbook, the mirror, and the view outside the window because you think that if you don't look at it anymore maybe the problem will cease to exist. That's why some pastors don't look at reports of the weekend attendance or the weekly offerings more than once a month, because things have not changed. Staff meetings and board meetings have become ad hoc because not much is happening and the meeting serves only as an inevitable reminder of what is not taking place rather than what should be happening.

Much like the widow, we become so defeated by circumstances that we've almost forgotten that the oil is in the pantry—there is still *something* left! Something is always better than nothing. One talent is always better than no talent at all. The oil before the miracle (because a miracle *is* coming) represents the remaining hopes, dreams, and resources that were once full but are now dwindling. Inevitably, as the supply dwindles so does vision. However, the oil can mean something totally different depending on how you see it. It can represent what you have, not what you don't have. For the widow, her answer to Elisha's question was the giveaway: "All I have is a little. . ."

Beyond Winepress Walls

When you are so up-close-and-personal to a problem, it's tough to see beyond it. When you have a front-row seat, your mind tells you to focus on what's in front of you rather than reaching for a glimpse of what lies beyond. Like Gideon (Judges 6) who is threshing wheat in a winepress, your view is limited because you can't see outside of the winepress. You can't seem to get ahead because there's no breeze, no wind to carry away the chaff and the rubbish of the kernels. It's clouding your vision from seeing the good stuff that the Lord has put at your feet. You get stifled and weary from the heat. And it's easy to imagine that the last place you want to be threshing wheat is in a closed-off, walled-off environment. In your frustration, you put that pitchfork under your chin, hands rested upon it and react the way Gideon did when he said to the Angel of the Lord, "Oh, really? Then where is this God my forefathers told me about? Where is He when you need Him?"

I say you need to get out of the winepress! Set yourself up on a hill, get to higher ground, and give yourself a fresh perspective so you can see what is at your

By focusing on her problems, she failed to see that what she had left was more than enough for God to use.

feet. Because what you get is what you get, but what you have is all He needs. Getting yourself up on a high place is much different from placing yourself on a high horse. Get up out of the winepress and get the perspective of higher ground.

It's Right Under Your Nose

Have you ever misplaced your wallet or keys, and (like me) announced to anyone in earshot, "I can't find it!" only to discover it right there, under your nose? If you have, I think we could be really good friends one day.

The widow overlooked what was right in front of her. Why? Because she was focused on her grief and inability to care for her sons. Who could blame her? But by focusing on her problems, she failed to see that what she had left was more than enough for God to use. Read her response once again, "All I have left...."

When we started HCWO, I would look at some of the more established and successful churches and get frustrated. In fact, it didn't just happen in the first year, but continued on for several years. I would look over the fence at the other guys and say, "Man, if we had leaders like that . . ." or "If we had a video and drama team like that . . ." and then I began to dismiss what the Lord had already given me. I was focusing on what I did not have. What I had to learn to do was look at what I was already blessed with. Then, we could get down to business and make the most of it.

I rarely get to see our University of Hawai'i Warriors football team play on Saturday evenings because of church. On occasion, though, I can get to a game. One of Hawai'i's greatest rivalries was with the Fresno State Bulldogs, previously coached by Pat Hill. Coach Hill is a throwback from a bygone era. He didn't just walk up and down the sideline during a game; he stalked it. He owned the side-line. His Fu Manchu mustache made him look like a walrus, and he had an expressive passion for the game that was worth the price of admission. With several bowl games under his belt, the overriding motto of the Bulldogs under Coach

Make your own grass green!

Hill's tenure had been "anytime, anyplace, anywhere." It's as if he was saying, "Bring it on! It doesn't matter who we end up playing: USC, Penn State, Alabama, we'll play 'em!" I loved that about Coach Hill.

But the one thing about Coach Hill that stood out to me most was a quote in our local newspaper several years ago. A reporter asked if bigger universities sought him out as a new head coach. Coach Hill responded, "Everyone asks me if the grass is greener on the other side of the fence, wondering if I ever think about moving on to greener pastures, or whatever that is. I figure, 'Make your own grass green!'"

I had that quote up on my home-office wall for several years. It is forever burned in my memory. Why? Because it contains the essence of the parable of the talents. *Make your own grass green!* Stop focusing on what you don't have and begin looking at what you do have and make the most of it because ultimately, *you get what you get!*

For the widow, it wasn't as simple as taking what little oil she had and manufacturing more oil. That wasn't in the equation because if it were, this desperate mama would've done that. What she needed was a man of God from the outside who came to help her see that what she had was "more than enough" in the hands of God. She needed perspective about God's love for her. God saw her condition and was about to pour out His own special favor and provision for her. He just wanted her to cooperate with Him in the miracle.

CHAPTER 10

THE ART OF THE START

Small Starts and Humble Beginnings

"And though your beginning was small,
your latter days will be very great."
Job 8:7 ESV

"Do not despise these small beginnings,
for the Lord rejoices to see the work begin."
Zechariah 4:10 NLT

Our first Sunday at the newly dubbed Hope Chapel West O'ahu was filled with well-wishers from HCKB, the forty who came with us, and the forty plus who were already part of the church when we arrived. I was nervous and excited about the service and the opportunity that the Lord entrusted to us. I don't recall that first sermon because it was quite a blur. However, I do remember gathering the entire team (the soon to be new core leadership team) at the church, thanking the Lord in prayer, and giving everyone a high five. The families that joined us from Hope Chapel Kane'ohe Bay made huge sacrifices to be a part of the team.

HUMBLE BEGINNINGS

My first office was amazing. It was beautifully furnished with an incredible array of books lining the wall-to-wall shelves and aisles. There was coffee, chicken quesadillas, and free Wi-Fi for Internet connection. Tons of people filed into my office every day, from ten in the morning until nine at night. It was rent-free, had decent bathrooms, and great plate-glass windows looking over the Waikele Shopping Center. We even had security guards! I felt so safe in my new digs. I'd tell the church, "If you want to meet with me, I'll be at my new office. It's just across the street there, in Borders bookstore."

Randy Kimura, the first person who committed to help us restart the church, and I had brand-new Sony Vaio laptops and Nextel cell phones. I had the latest Bible software loaded onto my computer, and there you go, we were ready and open for business. I continued to run the HCKB youth ministry from September until December, 2001, pulling double duty while restarting the church, as Randy handled the day-to-day operations. He was our first full-time employee. But after a few months we soon realized that we needed a place for me to study, since my home was thirty minutes away, and a place we could hold team meetings. God always provided for us. A good friend of mine owned a cabinet and window company and lent me space (rent-free) in the mezzanine above his offices in an industrial complex. He provided a desk and I bought

We began small, but we were thinking big.

myself a decent chair from Office Max and connected the landline directly to our own phone with the church number. In this new space we conducted team meetings, new believers' classes, youth ministry, and almost everything. By the end of the first year, the church had grown to about 250.

For the first few years, almost everyone on the team who wasn't a full-time employee of the church was given a monthly stipend. Others gave their time "unto the Lord" as volunteers. We began small, but we were thinking big. As a rule of thumb, Ralph taught me that from the church's total monthly income, no more than 40 percent should be dedicated to salaries and benefits. With that in mind, stipends and unto the Lord (free) compensation structures came into play. As I look back, I am so thankful for those who sacrificed time and resources to lay a great foundation for the church. Randy left a career in the insurance field to become our first employee, and he still serves on staff today, leading our Connect Ministry. He deserves the award for putting up with me the longest! In all seriousness, both he and I have grown tremendously in our different roles over the past ten years and I am so glad we are still a team. In fact, if I had to do it all over again, Randy is still one of the first people I'd ask to help me.

SMALL STARTS ARE GREAT STARTS

It's so easy to look at a well-running church, ministry, business, you name it, and come up with a plethora of misconceptions. For instance, people often look at who we've become and think we've had it easy. On occasion, people have called us a "golden child." They see our church of several thousand people but don't know we basically started off on a wing and a prayer. They see the conferences we host and our presence in the community and think we always had this. Not so. It took seven years to reach a thousand people in attendance. Not many know I struggled with my identity as a pastor and had to overcome huge insecurities and deal with fear of failure. They didn't see our Equip and Inspire Leadership Conference our first year when we barely could muster up two hundred people to attend *and pay* for admission. No, we didn't have it easy, but what we did have was favor—the favor of the Lord. I can't explain it fully, but I believe favor happens when someone is prepared to receive it. The diligence we all put into our efforts, I think, made us favorable.

Even so, in the beginning things weren't happening fast enough for me. It's as if the church was a little baby, and I would look at it crawling on the ground and complain, "When are you going to walk?" I'd wonder, *Why is it taking the baby so long to grow? Can't we do something to make her grow faster?*

Ridiculous, huh? But that is what I was doing to the church. I had to come to the realization, like I did with my daughters, that I needed to enjoy every developmental stage.

It doesn't help that I can be very competitive. It's hard to not look at how other churches are doing. With my competitive spirit, I knew it would become unhealthy for me to compare. Instead, I needed to learn how to admire and emulate. This can be challenging in its own right, though. If we have insecurities, or lack a healthy self-image, we resort to criticizing to somehow make us feel better. In the context of church leadership, we look at a larger church and say things like, "Oh, that church is so into numbers," or "They don't know how to disciple people." Knowing this, we needed to examine ourselves in the mirror and focus on how to reach our own unique potential.

Instead of coveting what other churches had accomplished, I decided I was going to learn from them. I enrolled at Pacific Rim Bible College (now Pacific Rim Christian College), a Bible college started by New Hope O'ahu. Classes in leadership and preaching were a tremendous help and added to the strong foundation I had received at HCKB. I began attending New Hope's leadership practicums. Instead of being intimidated by the church's size, I began to experience its ethos for myself and what makes it tick. I have caught two things from

I don't go anywhere as a critic. There are enough of those sitting in pews.

New Hope: magnitude and excellence. When I say magnitude, I am referring to size of vision. No one has built a church of its size in Hawai'i since the 1800s, when Haili Congregational Church blossomed during the Second Great Awakening.

I don't go anywhere as a critic. There are enough of those sitting in pews. And I completely believe Jesus' words when He said, "For in the same way you judge others, you will be judged, and with the measure you use, it will be measured to you" (Matthew 7:2). Even if I attend a workshop or conference in which I have a feeling it might not be as impacting as I would like, I pray for an open mind and open heart, waiting to receive what the Lord wants to download into me.

I believe one of the biggest deterrents to church growth can be a pessimistic attitude. If I ever showed up somewhere with my arms crossed and a look on my face that said, "This better be good," then I need to look out because Proverbs 16:18 says, "Pride goes before destruction." It really irritates me when I see this. First of all, a bad attitude is wrong because you bring no honor with you. I'm really big on honoring others. I want to honor you by paying close attention. I want to honor people regardless of what they can and cannot do for me. Honor always pays off. Secondly, with a "show me" attitude, you close yourself off to the *rhema* (or revelation) God wants to speak to you through a particular man or woman. Lastly, I believe it saddens the Lord when His children aren't open to learning from others.

ADDITION THROUGH MULTIPLICATION

There's a saying that values and principles are sometimes better caught than taught. I believe this can be a very accurate statement. The early years of our development as pastors and leaders were critical. I've estimated that I spent almost a thousand hours in staff and discipleship meetings with Pastor Ralph. As a result of those times of formal discipleship, combined with informal lessons while hanging out at Ralph's pool or working together on my car, my leadership ability and capacity grew. I have caught so much wisdom, and as a result I can use that same kind of wisdom to lead others.

Another great thing learned has been a mindset and philosophy of multiplication. Discipleship is inherently linked to multiplication. In the process of discipleship you're learning to follow Jesus' command to make disciples. Small groups are the main engine of discipleship. And from day one, we have used a small-group system that has been used for years at Hope Chapel.

Mentioned earlier, MiniChurch is based on Acts 2:42–47. There is no way we could have retained a "small church feel" without it. Through MiniChurch, we are able to disciple the church in weekly small groups where the important elements of life-on-life discipleship take place.

In a MiniChurch, you have all the elements of the Acts 2 Church. There's teaching, fellowship, breaking of bread, praising God, and prayer. These are the most important dynamics in which disciples are made. (Not to mention, food that everyone brings for a potluck!) We have each MiniChurch review the sermon from the weekend service and discuss two simple questions: "What did the Holy Spirit say to you through the message that is applicable to your life?" and "What are you going to do with it?" I suppose you could get fancier with it, but it really is that simple. We've learned how to reproduce the church, multiply leadership, and offer godly wisdom to the Body, minister to one another, function in the gifts of the Holy Spirit and more, all through the simplicity of a MiniChurch. Just as one church "births" another church, so do MiniChurches birth or multiply into other MiniChurches. You can read more about our philosophy on church multiplication by reading Ralph Moore's book, *How to Multiply Your Church.*[1]

A START IS A START

I might have discounted our start and seen it as rather weak compared to others. Some are blessed with starts and launched out with hundreds, some with paid staff, state-of-the-art video, lighting and sound systems—the works! Or, perhaps they begin as a satellite-campus site and then slowly the umbilical cord is cut and they are left freestanding and doing great. That's a great start! In fact, we intend to plant a few churches just like that. But you know how some are able to do it like that, right? Because they can. Because "to whom much is given much is required." These examples are of churches that are of the five-talent variety. Just as there are multiple ways to pastor and lead a church, there is also more than one way to plant a church.

Normally, a "start" is small and the odds seem to be stacked against you. Some of our guys read *The Prayer of Jabez* by Bruce Wilkinson over ten years ago, and little did we know that 1 Chronicles 4:9–10 would influence us so much.[2] Jabez' prayer was an over-the-top type of prayer. He had boldly asked God to "bless him indeed." The reason some would call this boldness is because many Christians today seem to shy away from asking God to bless them. Oh, we have no problem asking God to bless our food, to bless our day, and even to bless other people. But we believe we would be remiss or even offensive to the Lord if we asked Him to bless us the way Jabez asked. This was no ordinary blessing. According to Chuck Swindoll in his book *Fascinating Stories of Forgotten Lives*, Jabez was asking the Lord for an "uncommon blessing."[3]

But Jabez didn't stop there. He asked the Lord to "enlarge his territory;" to make him wealthy and prosperous, "to keep him from harm," and that he would not cause anyone "pain." I find this fascinating because of the start Jabez had. When his mother gave birth to him she gave him the name Jabez. The

We wrongly believe we would be remiss or even offensive to the Lord if we asked him to bless us the way Jabez asked.

meaning of his name originates from the word "pain." Imagine if your first name was *Pain*. What would growing up with a name like that do to you? I think we could all agree that his mother definitely gave him a name viewed as a curse and not a blessing.

Talk about a horrible start. However, the last part of verse 10 says, "And God granted his request." Now isn't this the underdog of all underdogs? Seriously, to be able to bounce back from a start like that is noteworthy, to say the least.

Think about it. Here's a guy who has one of the worst names in the Bible. But somehow he believes that it's perfectly fine for him to ask God to bless him with an uncommon blessing, to make him wealthy, to have God's hand on him at all times, and to keep him from causing pain the way his name implies. I love this guy! He is a biblical version of Hollywood's *Rudy*! I think the only other person in the Bible who gives Jabez a run for his money is Nabal, whose name when translated means "fool." What was wrong with their mothers?

The difference between these two guys is that one is blessed indeed and the other dies prematurely. We've all got a starting point. Don't be a hater of those who have had easier starts than you, because God knows what He's doing. If you've had a slow start or a struggling start or a small start, don't lose heart. The Lord knows what you're capable of doing.

I believe that the Lord loves all kinds of starts. If you've had a great start, you shouldn't feel guilty over it. Feeling guilty over a great start would be like a kid who grew up as a Christian, but as an adult looks back at his life and laments his unstained testimony because it lacks a dramatic conversion experience. Where is the guilt and shame in that? If you've had a great and fast start, congratulations! You have done well!

Maybe you were blessed with a slow start. That's right, blessed. The Lord knew you could handle it. Maybe God knew that the lessons you would glean from your start would encourage and inspire others who have had similar beginnings. As I look back, I wouldn't trade our start for anything else.

In the parable of the talents the man with the one talent could definitely be viewed as having the smallest start because he had the least amount given to him. Unfortunately he didn't see the power in what he was given. Too bad for him. If he had gotten over it and moved on in spite of having the slowest and smallest start, it is very likely that he would've succeeded.

REJOICE IN IT

When the people of Israel returned from seventy years of Babylonian captivity, they came back, as recorded in the Book of Ezra, to rebuild the Temple. The first Temple was magnificent! King Solomon spared no expense in creating an elaborate house of worship. But when Israel began their swift and steady decline away from worshipping God, He'd had enough. The Lord commissioned prophet after prophet to warn one king after another of their evil ways. They failed to repent. As a result, God stirred up a sleeping giant, the kingdom of Babylon. God's people were taken against their will and into exile. It was one of the most horrible times in Israel's history. Seventy years later, when the exiles returned from their captivity, the younger generation was finally able to see the site of the original Temple. What they saw was not the magnificent center of worship that they had heard about. It was nowhere near its former glory. What they saw were the ruins of a once proud center of worship and Jewish nationalism, the House of the Lord, now reduced to a pile of rubble.

So, they began to rebuild. However, when the old-timers realized that the new structure wouldn't come close to the former glory of the first Temple, they were extremely disheartened. Instead of rejoicing over the rebuilding of the new Temple, they turned it into a time of mourning. Yet the Lord, in His gentle way, sent the prophet Zechariah to encourage them saying, "Do not despise these small beginnings, for the Lord rejoices to see the work begin" (Zechariah 4:10 NLT).

The word *despise* in Hebrew is translated as to hold as insignificant, to hold in contempt, which gives us the idea of something being trampled under foot.[4] These men saw the new start of the Temple as insignificant, but the Lord rejoiced to see the start of something new. If you've had a small start, a slow

These men saw the new start of the Temple as insignificant, but the Lord rejoiced to see the start of something new.

start, or a struggling start, rejoice! Because if God saw that second Temple as being significant even with its small beginning, wouldn't He delight in the small beginning of your church? Isn't that amazing? It doesn't matter how big you are or how small you are. It doesn't matter if you've had a great start or small start. The bottom line is that you get a start.

How about you? Have you been looking down and despising the start you've been given? Are you ashamed of your humble beginnings? If you are, I hope you will look at where you are today and where you were yesterday and find joy in your humble beginning.

This is where it begins. Do the very best that you can with what you have been given and you will hear the words,

> *"Well done, good and faithful servant; you have been faithful over a few things, I will make you ruler over many things. Enter into the joy of your Lord."*

(Matthew 25:23 NKJV)

---

[1] Ralph Moore. *How to Multiply Your Church: The Most Effective Way to Grow God's Kingdom* (Regal, 2009).

[2] Bruce Wilkinson, *The Prayer of Jabez* (Multnomah, 2000).

[3] Chuck Swindoll, *Fascinating Stories of Forgotten Lives* (Nashville: Word Publishing, 2005).

[4] *Blue Letter Bible*. "Dictionary and Word Search for 'Despise' (Strong's 936)," 1996-2011.

CHAPTER 11

EQUIPPING A CONTENDER

Stewarding Well What Is Entrusted to You

"... I have not achieved it, but I focus on this one thing:
Forgetting the past and looking forward to what lies ahead,
I press on to reach the end of the race and receive the
heavenly prize for which God, through Christ Jesus, is calling us."
Philippians 3:13–14 NLT

Whenever you start a new church (or in our case, relaunch an existing church), different people join for different reasons. There are those who came with us from HCKB who lived near the church in Waikele. What piqued their curiosity was no longer having to make the thirty-minute drive to Kane'ohe every week. But I believe that when they began to see the possibilities of our church, they became enthused about being a part of what God was about to do.

Besides geographical reasons, some joined us simply to be a part of something fresh and new. What's funny is that we had no idea what kind of commitment would be required. Everyone who came with us was soon placed into leadership roles. Some led the children's ministry and some served on the set up team. A few led MiniChurches and became a part of the core leadership. It was exciting, laborious, but best of all, lots of fun. Though our numerical expansion was slow, I'm convinced our personal development was the bigger lesson. People were discovering gifts and abilities they never thought they had. I consider that one of the great things about church planting. We were growing at a decent pace. We were introducing people to Jesus. It was great to see people filling roles and finding fulfillment in them. These were some of the core people that helped us in our first few years.

Getting People Involved

I'm guessing what we've experienced at our church, especially with new people, isn't much different from what you've seen. Most people sincerely want to make a difference wherever they plant themselves in a church. But they don't think they're gifted enough to do a certain task, or traditional ministries within the church don't grab their interest. They see the worship team and think, *I can't do that.* They see the parking lot attendants, ushers, greeters, children's ministry workers, people in hospitality ministry, and think, *None of this interests me.*

If new people do want to volunteer, how many ushers or greeters are really needed? There are only so many of those positions to go around. As I said, though, lots of people tell themselves, *There's got to be more than this! More than*

✦

We were meant to flow like rivers, not store like reservoirs!

✦

just good music and good Bible teaching. Give me something to do. Help me make an impact. I love that!

Seriously, there are only so many classes you can take, sermons to podcast, books to read, and worship to listen to. Eventually, there has to be an outlet for all that input. We were meant to flow like rivers, not store like reservoirs! If there's no flow, you become like Israel's Dead Sea—full of deposits but lacking an environment for growth or life!

If people are growing in their relationship with Jesus and walking in the power of the Holy Spirit, they will eventually arrive at the point where they are searching to make a *significant contribution* to the lives of others. When they find what they were created to do, this brings glory to God. That's where personal fulfillment happens. That's their sweet spot. I'm not putting anyone down who's serving in the church in the "obvious" places—the parts of the Body that are seen, because I serve there too. I'm talking about discovering areas *outside* of the church for people to serve where they can make a significant contribution.

This is where the Church—my church, your church—has to provide ministry opportunities outside the Lord's house that stir people to action. This can only happen if people are being challenged and not coddled, and are presented opportunities to minister that are brought about by what Bill Hybels calls a *holy discontent.*[1] A person has holy discontent when there's something either tangible or intangible that is bothering them about their life, work or ministry. This, Hybels says, can be the fuel for personal or ministerial vision. I believe that holy discontent must receive the proper attention before you either lose your fire for it, or it grows to the point where it's out of control.

This holy discontent is where the potential lies inside a person to *do something* of significance.[2] I would consider this form of dissatisfaction as evidence of a *talent deposit* made by the Master. For instance, let's say you're sitting in church one weekend and are moved and stirred by the Holy Spirit through the teaching. The pastor begins speaking of your God-given calling and how you have a destiny to fulfill. You begin to get excited because there's a dream, a seed that lies dormant inside you. Situations and circumstances have come into your life that prevented you from fulfilling your God-given potential.

But now the preacher has just messed with your life! As I like to say here in Hawai'i, he has just *put his finger in your poi.*[3] In other words, he stuck his nose in your business. You have to do something about it. The question is: *How will you respond?* Will you walk out and ignore it (which, by the way, is a form of disobedience)? Or, will you face it and entertain the thought of what *could be* if you started to do something? There are myriads of people with untapped potential sitting in our churches every weekend. I love these people!

Of course in every church, you have those who will sit and just want to be "fed" like babies, get their Sunday service under their belt and move on for the rest of the week. They don't do much self-feeding during the week and their main meal is on Sunday. The sheep that eat once a week are what I call anorexic sheep. As a result, they become weak and feeble.

My philosophy is to let them sit for a while. If you're a pastor like me, you might be frustrated feeling as if you are entertaining them every week. Let them be. If they aren't ready to get involved yet, they aren't ready. However, one thing is for sure—they will either get tired of you challenging them every weekend to "do something" and they may leave, or they will be converted to your culture and eventually make a difference.

HOLD PEOPLE LOOSELY

As you well know, people leave churches for new ones. We didn't get a lot of transfer growth in the beginning, but through the years we've had our share. I know pastors who frown on this kind of growth. But the truth is, transfer growth is inevitable. It happens. People have all kinds of reasons for changing churches. There are the proximity reasons I mentioned earlier. We've had

We can't satisfy everyone and neither can your pastor and church.

people leave our church because they lived closer to another church, and saving time and gas money just made sense. I'll often recommend a church whose pastor I am friends with and encourage them to go and make the same, if not greater, contribution to that church.

People will leave one church for another because their children love the children's ministry at one place or their friends attend another. Others transfer because they begin to hear the "shepherd's" voice with more clarity at another church. When this happens and people leave (some you'll be glad to see go!),

115

deal with it. There could be some really good lessons to be learned when they leave. But at the end of the day, we can't satisfy everyone and neither can your pastor and church.

Not everyone who comes to our church is meant to stay. When it comes to hearing the voice of the Shepherd through a shepherd, one of the greatest lessons I learned was from Pastor Ralph. I was having difficulties with a woman who began to do things I could no longer tolerate in our church. I told Ralph about the situation and he suggested, "Tell her, with her husband present, 'Jesus said, "the sheep hear the shepherd's voice." Because you are no longer listening to me, you have disqualified me as your shepherd. I'm sure that there is another in whom you will hear the chief Shepherd's voice. I am now releasing you to go find that shepherd through whom you can hear the voice of the Lord.'"

This lesson taught me to hold people loosely. One thing I have learned as a pastor is that Lisa and I don't own anyone. People are free to come and go as they please. It doesn't mean my feelings won't be hurt if certain people end up leaving, or if they leave with unsettled issues. But this lesson has allowed me to help others find a congregation they can truly belong to. We've learned to hold people loosely. Now don't get me wrong, staff members are a different story. I've had a few occasions where a staff member or two were recruited to join another church without me knowing it, and I was naturally disappointed.

When it comes to staff members on our team, here's what I believe—if you treat people well and they know you genuinely care for them and their family, they will stay. If you compensate them honorably, and you have a vision that is inspiring enough to follow, they will flourish.

Sure, there are exceptions. When a person believes the Lord has truly called them to go to another place, who can argue with that? I want God's best for everyone, including for our church. So if God's best for someone is to go elsewhere, benefitting them greatly, I have to believe that God is looking out for my best interests and our church's interests. I found that when I have this outlook, it often turns into a win-win situation for everyone. That's how the Kingdom should operate. Hold them loosely.

Hidden Agendas

If you are a pastor, there are a few things to consider when new people join your church. Sometimes those who transfer from another church carry with them discontent, dissatisfaction, frustration and other unresolved issues. There are even times when people will be frustrated with my leadership or that of another pastor's. If this is brought to my attention, a couple of things need to take place: First, a conversation, and second, an eventual conclusion. In the case of those who leave other churches because they are dissatisfied, each should be carefully considered and discernment from God must be employed.

When you're young and green, some will make the mistake of thinking they can influence you. This is where you have to be very careful. They may try and influence you or others to gain an audience or favor in their direction. This could be a demonic plan. One of the men I admire, Paul Risser, former president of the Foursquare denomination, once told me, "God has a plan for your church just like He has a plan for your life. But the other thing you need to know is that the enemy also has a plan for your life as well as a plan for your church. So, sometimes he will plant people in your church, good people who don't realize that they're being used this way, to distract and disrupt you from what the Lord is trying to do through your church and through you."

Stewarding People

It goes without saying that those who are first-time decision makers for Christ are the best kind of growth. I also love people who are returning to the Lord after backsliding. We contend for salvations every weekend at HCWO. Rarely a service goes by on a weekend where an altar call isn't given. We want the people in our church to expect an altar call, so if they bring a friend, family member, or someone with whom they've been sharing their faith, there's a great chance that they'll respond to Jesus after hearing a very clear and straightforward presentation of the Gospel. Giving altar calls is a stewardship issue. If you're not giving altar calls, you're not stewarding your talents well.

117

As a pastor, stewarding people is much the same as stewarding talent. It is to be taken seriously. As in the parable of the talents, we could lose precious people if we do not shepherd or steward them well. Every person must be

⟡

If you're not giving altar calls, you're not stewarding your talents well.

⟡

important to us. For this cause, I feel such a strong responsibility and burden to ensure that the altar call is clear and that we have thorough follow-up to ensure they grow deep roots and bear fruit in the Lord.

In the earlier days of the church, we didn't take as focused an approach as we do now. Today, when someone surrenders their life to Jesus, we have them stand where they are and repeat the prayer of salvation in public. Why this new approach? I feel that if they can make a stand in a place as safe as church then they'll be able to stand firm when persecution for their faith comes; because we all know, it comes. After they've prayed to surrender their lives to Jesus, I explain that we will walk them out to the lobby where our Connect Pastor will clearly explain what just took place, what their next steps are, and give them a Bible. We have "counselors" there to pray with them, then we assign a person who will walk them through their next steps.

I want to make sure we are doing all we can, the best we can, to steward these new believers. I don't want to take their decision to follow Jesus lightly. In Jesus' parable of the four soils found in Luke 8:4–15, the farmer scattered seed on four types of soil. The seeds that fell on the footpath lay exposed, were trampled on by foot, and later eaten by birds. Jesus explained that these seeds represented those who heard the message and understood its meaning, but soon the devil arrived and snatched away the Word planted in their hearts, thus preventing them from believing and being saved.

Other seeds fell amongst rocks, which began growing at first, but soon withered and died because there wasn't enough moisture to nourish them. These people, Jesus pointed out, received the message with great joy at first! They were excited and believed for a while but because they didn't allow their roots to grow

118

deep, they fell away when they encountered temptation. Lured back by their old sinful ways, they too withered and faded away. I have seen this happen far too many times. They get so excited about Jesus; they have a clean slate and are now on the right path. But because they don't get grounded in the Word of God and are not connected to the church family, they fall away. Tragic.

Jesus then explained that other seed fell among thorns, which represent the cares and riches of the world. These thorns overpowered the message and crowded out any chance of growth. They represent people who hear the Word, receive it, but succumb to their old sinful nature and satisfy themselves on what the world presents as priorities; having more and experiencing more to the point where the "more" overcomes them and is their undoing.

But the last type of seed that fell on fertile soil had the best chance of survival and did more than survive! Jesus said they were people who received the Word of God with right hearts, clung to it and slowly and patiently grew to produce a huge harvest!

According to this parable, only a fraction of those who hear the Word actually receive the Word. If we also take into consideration the account of the parable of the wheat and weeds in Matthew 13:24–30, where the enemy plants weeds among the wheat while the farmer is asleep, you can see why I think every church should have a renewed emphasis to keep those we reach. By no means do we have this down to a science, but we must contend to do the best we can with those the Lord has entrusted to us.

---

[1] Bill Hybels, *Holy Discontent* (Grand Rapids, MI: Zondervan, 2007).

[2] Miles McPherson, *Do Something: Make Your Life Count* (Grand Rapids, MI: Baker Books, 2009).

[3] Poi is a Hawaiian staple, similar to what potatoes mean to caucasians from the U.S. mainland, and rice to those of Asian cultures. Poi is often served at parties in Hawai'i where Hawaiian food is served.

CHAPTER 12

HARDWORKING HYBRIDS

Being the Best at Who You Were Called to Be

"The plans of the diligent lead surely to advantage,
But everyone who is hasty comes surely to poverty."
Proverbs 21:5 NASB

"Careful planning puts you ahead in the long run;
hurry and scurry puts you further behind."
Proverbs 21:5 The Message

In the first years of HCWO, we worked hard. Hard work is what it really takes to have a thriving church. Hands down, leading a church of any size is a great endeavor. Through hard work and the help of the Holy Spirit, we set out to build a great church. We didn't want to build a mediocre church, a so-so church, or a "decent" church; we wanted to build a great church. To me, a great church is where people are getting saved every weekend and great unity exists between believers. It's also a place where people are set free and healed from all kinds of ailments, and the power of the Holy Spirit is flowing. Additionally, a great church, in my mind, is naturally supernatural (not weird).

It's a place where disciples are being developed and people are discovering gifts and talents. It's a place where dreams rekindle and everyone is finding their purpose and destiny in life. In this great church, children and teens enjoy church, not just endure it. Families become stronger, single parents find strength and remarry, and divorced couples find hope. Worship is amazing in the kind of

Whatever your occupation or whatever season you are in, don't wait for the "whens."

church I envision. In the church we set out to build, believers join together in small groups to pray for, encourage and exhort one another. In this church, the End-Times Harvest would be of the highest priority and churches would inevitably be planted to the glory of God. There would be *life* in this church!

We set out to build a great church at *every level!* We didn't just sit back and say, "When we get bigger, then we will. . . ." No. It was more like, "Let's be the best in our weight-class!" Whatever your occupation or whatever season you are in, don't wait for the "whens." You know, the "when we make it" or "when we have more money" or "when I get out of this place." If it's a good thing you hope to be, be it now. Too many times in my past I found myself putting off things to the *when* stage of life. Sometimes, the when will never come unless you start acting like it, or do something about it now.

EXPONENTIAL GROWTH FOLLOWS

In the parable about the talents, remember how the master says to his servant, "You were faithful over a few things, I will make you ruler over many things"? (Matthew 25:21 NKJV). From the very beginning we have been determined to be faithful with the few God has entrusted to us. The master's words to his servant match our experience: exponential growth doesn't begin until incremental growth has occurred. For instance, if we were to map out our growth from the first year up until today, we would see growth from 60 to more than 3,200 each weekend in eleven years. From a bird's-eye view, that looks like we were on the fast-track! But if you look at the first eight years, you'd notice it was incremental growth. We went from 80 in 2001 to 1,000 at the beginning of 2009. If we were to calculate an average it would look like 15 to 20 percent growth every year until 2009. In all of those eight years, we worked very hard and were very diligent to do the best we could with what we had been given.

A month-to-month view of our growth chart for the first eight years shows growth, plateaus, dips, another plateau, a sharp increase (Easter or Christmas), another plateau, and then a slight dip again. We've experienced months when I'd think to myself that if things didn't swing, we would be in trouble!

This is what it means to have incremental growth. We grew in increments in the first eight years because we focused on simple goals. They were prayerful goals, mind you. Proverbs 21:5 (TLB) says, "Steady plodding brings prosperity. . . ." Our goals were simple: add more MiniChurches every quarter, reach more people through salvations every weekend, and get better at what we do in every area. We simply thought that if we could improve in every area (after evaluating all areas of the ministry), we were headed in the right direction. Now, Eeyore from *Winnie the Pooh* would have said, "Oh, we're just plodding along." But I'd say it was more like a *prevailing* plodding. We kept plodding in the right direction, and I believe it was this type of consistency that set the stage for God to bring EXPONENTIAL growth, which we are still experiencing!

There were times we were tempted; lured off the *prevailing plodding path* to different directions. "This church" or "that conference" would offer an enticing formula for success. There is so much to choose from. There were many different kinds of "wineskins" we could have modeled ourselves after. But after experimenting with a few, we decided we would be the best at who we were. Discovering that was really easy. We were, after all, a Hope Chapel. There are certain core values that make a church a Hope Chapel church. We never strayed from that. But as we grew, we began adding new components to the DNA we already had.

HYBRID . . . IT'S A GOOD THING

When I mentioned that people criticize what they don't understand, I have first-hand experience. I normally would hesitate to share some of the opposition we encountered, but I believe what I share may help someone. Some of the criticism we would receive from pastors would be, "You're not a real Hope Chapel." When I would hear this, I would ask, "Tell me, what's a Hope Chapel to you?" The funny thing is, they could not put their finger on it. Then they'd say, "Oh, HCWO, you're a hybrid."

In general usage, *hybrid* was first used to describe the offspring of animals of differing breeds or in the combining of separate plants in horticulture. Today, most of us know a hybrid as a car that runs partly on electricity and partly on gasoline. When hybrid vehicles first entered car showrooms they were deemed unusual and received much criticism and speculation by the public. When we were referred to as "the hybrid church," I did not receive it as a compliment at first. I bristled at the description. But then of course, I would consider the source.

If being a *hybrid* meant I had brought home principles and inspiration that resonated with me from conferences abroad or churches in Hawai'i, and that made us a hybrid—then yes, we are a *hybrid*. If it meant we already had the DNA of a Hope Chapel, much like how every car has a chassis and four tires, and we just added some things or got better as a result of studying other ministries, then yes, guilty as charged: *hybrid!* If it meant that I read books and learned so much from them that we implemented some of the principles we learned which helped our church, then like the movie *The Elephant Man,*[1] I confess, "I am not an animal, I am . . ." a *hybrid!* If it meant I was not satisfied with all that I knew—that I had a hunger to see things I had never seen before and wanted to catch the culture of ministries that were far beyond ours—then *hybrid* me!

Do we have the foundation of Hope Chapel and do we multiply disciples and plant churches? You bet your new Justin Bieber hairdo we do! (Coincidentally, it's just a remake of the late Roy Orbison's wig.) Do we enjoy Hillsong's songwriting and emulate their worship style? Most definitely! Besides, it's not that hard to play their music. And, we now write *our own* songs, multiplying the talent the Lord entrusted to us. Did the excellence of New Hope O'ahu influence our overall presentation? What do you think? Ironically, now they send their teams to see how and what we do! Isn't that great? If that's what it means to be a hybrid, then I wholeheartedly admit it: we are a hybrid! You can call us anything you want as long as you don't call us lazy. The amazing thing about hybrid vehicles today is that they have opened up a whole new market in the auto industry. They are even considered in a class all by themselves. I just have one thing to say: *Hybrid!*

STRETCH AND FLEX

Yes, we are a hybrid and we're proud of it. We have taken the best of what we have seen and added it to who we already were. Call it what you will. I call it stewardship. We are not content to be the same church until Christ returns.

We contend to keep the same values of an Acts 2, New Testament church, but we will continue to morph into what we sense the Lord calling us to be. When it comes to remaining flexible, I love what Paul said in 1 Corinthians

> We have taken the best of what we have seen and added it to who we already were.

9:22, "I have become all things to all people so that by all possible means I might save some." I love his heart! There is a humility in *adapting* to change that is essential to a church. We must be willing to flex.

I have a saying that I've adjusted over the years regarding flexibility: "Blessed are the flexible for they will never be bent out of shape." This could be applied to our attitudes. But I also apply this to the church. We have to keep the "wineskin" of our church and lives flexible. If we are pliable, moldable, and shapeable, we can do anything and become anything so that we "might save some." Isn't that what it is all about, to save more people?

If we believe we are called to be fishers of men and not keepers of the aquarium, then it is imperative we remain flexible. When you remain inflexible you cannot retain new ideas, your wineskin cannot adjust and change, and the end result can be losing your effectiveness as a church. It's about stewardship. Flexibility will allow you to stretch as you discover your "new normal." When you've stretched to a new point, that new point of flexibility allows you to work from a new stage of development. When you are flexible you can stretch to work hard and take on more.

HARD WORK

Lisa and I were at a fundraiser one night where a large donor to the Pacific Rim Christian College was in attendance. This was no ordinary donor. This man was large himself. He had to be six-foot-five and someone said 250 pounds. I think he was more like 350. The emcee invited Ma'ake Kemoeatu to the podium. Hailing from Kahuku High School on the North Shore of O'ahu, Ma'ake was a walk-on (non-scholarship) football player (that's gridiron to the Aussies) to the University of Utah and currently on contract for the Baltimore Ravens as a defensive lineman. Ma'ake's brother, Chris, is a two-time Super Bowl player who was with the Pittsburgh Steelers. Must be nice to be Ma'ake and Chris' parents!

Interestingly enough, Kahuku High School was featured in *USA Today* several years ago as producing the most professional football players in the NFL than any other school per capita.[2] This is an amazing feat considering the enrollment of Kahuku High (about 1,000 from grades 9–12) is in a rural community with a population base of just under 20,000 people. That is an amazing accomplishment!

Anyway, while at the fundraiser, Ma'ake responded to a question the emcee asked him about his dedication to succeed when he was neither recruited nor drafted to the sport in which he now earns millions a year. He said, "Hard work beats out talent when talent doesn't work hard." It sounds so simple yet is so profound. In other words, if you work hard, you can join and outperform the person who has all the talent in the world, yet takes it for granted and cruises. That is what I call steady plodding!

The steady plodding of our ministry wasn't all about weekend services. There were people to care for and MiniChurches to increase and multiply. There were people to be discipled and leaders to be trained. Yes, we put lots of energy and creativity into getting the most out of our weekends. We had great people with great talent, but they weren't in abundance. What we did have in abundance were great people with great hearts, and with that you can certainly accomplish anything. Why? Because regardless of skill level, if they have the heart to serve and if they know it's not about them, then they are absolutely teachable. With their teachability we were able to take what they had been given and help them multiply their talents for the Lord. This is another thing I've discovered: the key to helping people become better is to engage their passions.

For those who worshipped with all of their heart in the congregation on Sunday, we'd try to find out if their voice was at the least halfway decent. If they were, we'd ask them to pray about joining the team. If they did, we'd invest in voice lessons. We weren't necessarily looking for another Chris Tomlin or Darlene Zschech. Don't get me wrong; we would take them in a New York minute! But what we were after was *the heart of the worshiper* that would help lead others into the presence of God. If we were to sit around and wait for a five-talent worship leader to appear at our door, we'd have been waiting for a long time! I believe we have our current worship leaders (and other types of leaders, for that matter) because we have been faithful with who have been given to us from day one. Someday, the world might be talking about a Koa Siu or a Cindy Scullard, just two of our gifted worship leaders with great potential for impact. But before they arrived, we had faithful leaders in Jonah Ka'auwai, Randall Kalama, Rodney Arias, Mike Chang, Frank De Gracia, and Melissa Matsuda, just to name a few. Each one gave us all they had. Most are still with us and a few have moved on to help other churches.

BEATS, RHYTHMS, AND SEASONS

I love music. In addition to worship music, I also love R&B and some Top 40. I love hearing the rhythm of a new song or the beat of an old one. And for a semi-white boy (the Italian side of me), I can dance too. I'm a quarter Filipino mixed with a quarter Italian with Hawaiian and Chinese, so I like to think I can dance the hula, sing like Pavarotti, dance like a Filipino, and possess the *Shaolin* skills like Bruce Lee. It takes coordination for martial arts, you know!

In life and ministry, I've had to constantly discover and adjust my rhythm. Finding the rhythm in ministry is important. If we aren't in the rhythm we've got to check on the beat. Is the beat too fast or too slow? Am I weary because I haven't found the right rhythm? Then get back to the right beat. I've heard it said, "Don't confuse the rhythm of a beat with a groove. The beat stays the same, but the groove is always changing." Therefore, the beat is like a metronome. A metronome is a musical device used to keep musicians in the right timing of a song. You have the control of setting the beat to how fast or

You have the control of setting the beat to how fast or slow you want to go.

slow you want to go. It's constant; it doesn't change unless you change it yourself. So you set the beat. Fortunately, as the senior pastor of the church, I can set the beat. If I'm in tune with what the Holy Spirit is doing in the church, the beat is set accordingly. Once we set the beat, we settle into a rhythm.

The church has a rhythm to it. Have you found your rhythm, or are you finding it quite erratic and unpredictable? Are you having problems keeping pace with the rhythm? Then adjust the beat. One of the best things we discovered was the rhythm of our church and how we respond to it. We likened our rhythm to a "season." For example, we have different seasons in church-life that I've adapted from the church of my close friend, Pastor Roger Archer, in Puyallup, Washington.

IGNITE, GROWTH, COMPRESSION, REGROUP

The first season is called *Ignite*. Ignite happens from August until December. It's the season when people come back to church from the summer and things seem to get started, much like a car is ignited from the spark plugs in its engine. The rhythm of people getting back to school, ending vacations, and families moving to O'ahu for one reason or another, also translates to growing church attendance and an increased amount of salvations. So things are ignited around our church and we will groove to that rhythm. We also start our church fiscal year in August to reflect the beginning of the seasonal year with Ignite.

The next season is called *Growth*. This season lasts from January until Easter weekend. There is evangelistic growth during this time. People are already thinking in late December about New Year's resolutions, turning over a new leaf and fresh starts for the year, and that translates into going to church. As a result, there are tons of opportunities to lead others to Christ. We experience a sharp increase in salvations in our weekend services from January until mid-March. Although there is salvation growth, things aren't as consistent as we would like them to be. I will never really know why as much as 20 to 30 percent of our church, on any given Sunday, will not be at church. I would love it if everyone showed up at the same time! Wouldn't that be great? But that rarely ever happens. Oh well.

The third season we've discovered is called *Compression*. Compression is like a flour sifter. Ever bake a pie? I have. Grandma Patsy taught me how to make pie crust. One of the things you had to do while sifting the flour was hit the sides of the sifter to get the flour that was on the wall of the sifter to fall into the meshing. It was a pretty constant slapping of the sifter. Compression is the shortest of seasons because it lasts from Easter until June first. Why? In this season, you'll discover who will be with you after an amazing Easter weekend. It's as though a sifting occurs during this time and who you're left with is who you'll be running with.

This all leads us to the final season in the twelve months of the church calendar, and it's called *Regroup*. Regroup is from June to August. This is a season when people of the church go on vacations, so we slow things down by resetting the metronome of church life to a much slower beat. Instead of flying in fifth gear, we downshift to fourth gear and get out of the fast lane on the left and cruise in the old lady lane to the far right of the expressway. This allows the church to rest and the staff to take their vacations and everyone to regroup and get ready for Ignite all over again.

One thing that is important to take into consideration: we don't do the same activities in every season. For instance, most of our evangelistic outreaches take place in Ignite because this is when seed is planted. The seed takes a while to grow and they will come to fruition during Growth, which is when the harvest comes in the heaviest. Of course we never tell our people to stop sharing their

Hard work, consistency, prevailing plodding—these are the keys to building a strong foundation.

faith in any season, but as far as any outreach events go, they are heaviest in Ignite. Additionally, during Growth, we place a stronger emphasis on discipleship courses and classes during this season. However, we do offer these types of classes year-round.

Hard work, consistency, prevailing plodding—these are the keys to building a strong foundation of incremental growth. Find a good rhythm that can sustain you for the long haul and you've got what it takes.

BLESSED TO BE A BLESSING

Ever wonder why pastors and other leaders generally work so hard? Do we work hard for a blessing? Or are we just blessed? Is it by faith or works? There are those who feel God sovereignly chooses to bless whom and what He so desires. I believe that. We have all seen it happen in different areas of business and ministry. God's hand seems to be prospering and blessing someone and it just seems like it was "so easily" handed to them on a silver platter. However, I feel that sentiment is incomplete.

From my vantage point, in His sovereignty, the Lord blesses those who are faithful to Him. In 2 Chronicles 16:9 (NASB) it says, "For the eyes of the Lord move to and fro throughout the earth that He may strongly support those whose heart is completely His." God is searching to bless those whose hearts are fully committed to Him. Being committed to Him is also being committed to what we call "the things of God." Those *things* include what has been entrusted and given to us. Therefore, if we are faithful to the things God has given to us, He seeks us out (the faithful), to strengthen (show strong support) to those who are fully committed to Him.

Faith and works go hand in hand. God does His part, we do ours. We are co-laborers in and with Christ. His blessings don't negate our action but neither are His blessings earned. They are simply that—a blessing! When our lives are fully His we can understand that we are indeed blessed to be a blessing.

Incremental growth is a great blessing. Stay the course and keep at it. Steady plodding in the same direction brings great results. Whether the exponential factor kicks in or not, it's still something to cheer about. I'm not guaranteeing your church will double; that's up to God. But I am sure that preparing faithfully in these things sets the stage for exponential growth. And if it arrives, be ready for it. Because you never know when growth will turn in your favor in an exponential way!

---

[1] David Lynch, director, *The Elephant Man*, 1980.

[2] Sal Ruibal, Tiny Hawai'i Looms as Giant in Football World, *USA Today*, http://www.usatoday.com/sports/football/2004-11-09-hawaii-football_x.htm.

CHAPTER 13

BRING IT!

Your Contribution to the Fight

"Well, my brothers and sisters, let's summarize. When you meet together, one will sing, another will teach, another will tell some special revelation God has given, one will speak in tongues, and another will interpret what is said. But everything that is done must strengthen all of you."

1 Corinthians 14:26 NLT

Within our first year, the Lord gave me a strategy and a philosophy of ministry from the Book of Acts. Every church-planter and pastor knows that Acts 2:42–47 is the foundational bedrock model for the New Testament church:

"They devoted themselves to the apostles' teaching and to fellowship, to the breaking of bread and to prayer. Everyone was filled with awe at the many wonders and signs performed by the apostles. All the believers were together and had everything in common. They sold property and possessions to give to anyone who had need. Every day they continued to meet together in the temple courts. They broke bread in their homes and ate together with glad and sincere hearts, praising God and enjoying the favor of all the people. And the Lord added to their number daily those who were being saved."

Acts 2:42–47

Even though this passage is well known, it's beneficial to look at it closely again. When Jesus left this earth and ascended back to heaven, He told His faithful followers (who numbered about 120) to wait for the promise of the Holy Spirit. Acts 1:8 records the event: "But you will receive power when the Holy Spirit comes on you; and you will be my witnesses in Jerusalem, and in all Judea and Samaria, and to the ends of the earth." So, that's what they did. They prayed and waited for Jesus' promise to be fulfilled. On the Day of Pentecost (a Jewish holiday), while the 120 were in the Upper Room praying and waiting for the

The Church multiplied greatly as the apostles and believers interacted with God like never before.

promise, the Holy Spirit suddenly filled them and they poured out into the streets of Jerusalem praising God in languages they had never learned. Amazingly, they were understood by pilgrims of far-off lands who were in the city celebrating Pentecost. This occasion is known as the birth of the Church.

In a brief matter of time, the Church multiplied greatly as the apostles and believers interacted with God like never before in the history of God's people. In the Old Testament days the third person of the Trinity (the Holy Spirit) would "come upon" a favored person and endow them with supernatural power and ability from the *outside*. But here in the New Testament, every believer was filled with the Holy Spirit from the *inside*. The Church exploded with supernatural power and exponential impact. The rest is history. Acts 2:42–47 is the record of how the early Church operated and it continues to be the blueprint that most churches today, including ours, build with.

There are eight things we can gather from this passage:

1. *"They devoted themselves to the apostles' teaching."* This is discipleship. Followers were becoming disciples of Jesus Christ through the apostles' teaching.
2. *". . . And to fellowship."* They interacted with one another on an intimate and spiritual level as brothers and sisters in Jesus.

3. *". . . To the breaking of bread."* They celebrated communion together as the Lord commanded in His last meal with His disciples as recorded in Luke 22:19, and confirmed by Paul the Apostle in his letter to the church in Corinth in 1 Corinthians 11:24.
4. *". . . And prayer."* Jesus told His disciples that His house would be a "house of prayer" in Matthew 21:13.
5. *". . . Filled with awe at the many signs and wonders."* They experienced the supernatural power of the Holy Spirit.
6. *". . . All the believers . . . had everything in common . . . To give to anyone in need."* The first church shared and cared for the needs and welfare of all.
7. *"They broke bread in their homes and ate together with glad and sincere hearts."* These disciples ate a lot, had a lot of fun and were filled with the joy of the Lord.
8. *"And the Lord added to their number daily those who were being saved."* The church was reaching lost people.

With this Scripture in mind, I remember asking the Lord for a mission statement. I felt tremendous pressure to craft one because that was what all the books on church growth said we needed to have. Did I really? Mission statements, purpose statements, vision statements, and value statements—they were so overwhelming! In the beginning, we borrowed a few because, truthfully, I had no idea where to start! But then the Lord gave me an idea. As a former youth pastor, "acrostic" was my name, and making phrases out of letters was my game! Any youth pastor worth his salt can work with an acrostic. So I decided to take the word *Acts*, and made it ACTS: Attract, Connect, Train, and Send.

Attract is for evangelism. *Connect* involves fellowship and assimilation of the saved into the life of the church. *Train* is another word for equip as in "to equip the saints for the work of ministry" as stated in Ephesians 4:12 (ESV). Lastly, *Send* refers to those we train, equip, and commission into the world to do what Jesus called us to do, which is to "make disciples of all nations." There we have it: ACTS—a strategy, a philosophy of ministry, and a concise mission statement all rolled into one.

What makes me really excited about ACTS is the *Send* element. Most Christians assume that being "sent" means leaving everything behind, and becoming a missionary or a church-planter. The fact of the matter is that not everyone is called to be a missionary or a pastor. With that in mind, the Lord impressed upon me that we were to help people realize their dreams and God-given calling—we are called to help them achieve these. Then they would be "sent" to fulfill His plans and desires for their lives.

THE MYTH OF THE "2-PERCENT CALLING"

What typically happens in a church is people are often hesitant to move to the next stage of the assimilation process. Many stop at the Attract stage or the Connect stage without progressing to the next level. This results in even less people who feel the calling to move through Train into Send. Why are they stuck

❧

The fact of the matter is that not everyone is called to be an overseas missionary or a pastor.

❧

between Connect, Train, or Send? Because they have a traditional view of what it means to be called and sent by the Lord. Many believe that only those who are pastors or missionaries—roughly 2 percent of the church—fall into the category of those who have been called to be sent. I call this myth the "2-percent calling."

Most Christians have a pretty clear understanding regarding the basic call of God for believers. This basic call involves the call to evangelize, to live a life that honors God, and to cultivate their relationship with God and others. But if we were to ask the average Christian what their personal, God-given destiny/calling/purpose is, I would venture to guess that most don't really know or think that they qualify for one. With the old paradigm in mind, my concern lay with the 98 percent who feel they were not given the 2-percent calling. In order to empower the remaining 98 percent, we decided to approach the whole evangelism-assimilation-equipping process differently. We needed to look at it from a radically different angle.

We began with the understanding that everyone who has come to our church is drawn by the Holy Spirit, and the conviction that we needed to steward well those who the Lord was entrusting to us—all 100 percent. We refused to give in to the myth of the 2-percent calling. We asked ourselves, "What if everyone we attracted got connected to a MiniChurch, a ministry, or a serving opportunity? And what if all those who got connected were trained and equipped each week? What would that look like for the church?" That would be incredible! If we can get the 98 percenters to see that they have a calling as well—there is no telling what God can do with a church like that!

ACTS

You might be thinking that this seems a little utopian. I understand. However, since I am under the conviction that everyone is called by God to do something of great significance, I believe every person can fulfill the *Send* category in ACTS. This ACTS concept that I have just shared with you has radically changed the culture of our church. No longer are the majority of people coming through our doors with an attitude of "okay, this better be good" or with a lackadaisical approach. It's more like, "I can't wait to see what God is going to

Attract, Connect, Train, Send—ACTS. It's more than just a concept. It works.

do and say today." Why the change? I believe the key is that we have intentionally created a culture in which everyone knows they are being equipped to be sent for the purpose of fulfilling their destinies; all 100 percent of them. Attract, Connect, Train, Send—ACTS. It's more than just a concept. It works.

People will constantly tell us that it feels different in our place. It's a good kind of different. I often credit this to our intercessory prayer ministry and the presence of the Holy Spirit. But I would be mistaken if I did not mention that it is also because people enter the parking lot on the weekends with a sense of anticipation—that

God is in the House and He's about to speak to them and they will have an encounter with Him. And when you have that level of expectation in the environment, combined with the presence of God, anything can happen!

Not only has this concept changed our church, it has changed the way I preach on weekends. In every sermon I'm looking for a "Send" element or example. I have two priorities in my sermons: The first is to include a call to salvation at the end of nearly every sermon. The second is to communicate that they are *called to be sent*. Whenever a mindset is adjusted, inevitably action will follow and new ideas will be implemented.

This new idea we were given, ACTS, was just what our church needed. We got it from the Lord. It wasn't developed on the spot or overnight. It was something that was refined over time and became what it is today after a lot of sifting. Friends, if the Lord ever gives you something like this, something that is not yet complete but has a lot of promise and potential, treat it like gold! It could very well be a talent deposit that the Lord is making into your account. Steward it well because what you do with it will make a huge difference in what you could be getting in the future.

Bring Your Dish

Throughout the formative years of HCWO, several analogies have served as visuals to help clarify the culture of our church. These analogies help us communicate who we are, who we intend to become, and what our expectations are.

One of these analogies has to do with food. As in most cultures, we in Hawai'i love our potlucks. I'm partial to Hawai'i potlucks because they're the best in the world. (With the exception of youth ministry potlucks. If you're in youth ministry, you know what I'm talking about. Sometimes students would forget to inform their parents, their source of all good things to eat, so we often ended up subsidizing our gatherings with extra rice, more main dishes ordered from the Korean Bar-be-que restaurant and cheap pizza.) True Hawai'i potlucks are special because of the diversity of ethnic groups represented in our great state.

To draw on the analogy of the potluck as it pertains to the church, everyone who comes to a potluck brings a dish because we all know that it's not proper to show-up at a potluck gathering without one. Generally, for the sake of the illustration, you would bring to the table a dish that represents your ethnicity and family. So if you are of Hawaiian descent, you would bring some poke[1] and kalua pig.[2] If your ethnic background is Japanese, you might bring a sushi platter. A family from the South might bring barbecued ribs and chicken. I'm sure you get the picture! When everyone brings a dish to the party, there is sure to be more than enough for everyone. Now that's a potluck!

At a potluck, the host welcomes everyone in. There is much fellowship, some music, the host blesses the food and then it's time to eat. There is barely enough room on the table for every dish presented. The women and children go first. Then, it's time for the men! After everyone goes through the food line, plates are heaped with food that peaks like a mountain at the top. Some with heartier appetites are more than happy to help themselves to seconds.

The house is filled with joy because of all the great food and fellowship. But the beautiful part is not just the variety and colors that cover the dining room table and countertops. It is more about the love and fellowship that fill the air.

Church should be like a potluck, not a restaurant.

Everyone feels good because they did not show up empty-handed. They were invited to come and encouraged to *bring something*. Without the people or their dishes, something would be missing. However, the true blessing of the potluck comes out when it's time for everyone to leave and head home.

After announcing your departure, the host will inevitably say, "Make a plate. Please. There's so much food and we can't eat it all. Take some for tomorrow's lunch! Make a plate." And, coming from our culture in Hawai'i, everyone will say, "Nah, I'm full. I can't eat another bite." But undeterred, the host will ask you, in fact exhort you twice more with, "Nonsense! Make a plate." And, because of his or her persistence, you'll give in and say, "Alright," and that's what you'll do, make a plate or two. Plates covered in tin foil will be placed in your clean casserole dish, which has been washed and dried. You head home with a clean serving dish and lots of leftovers.

Church should be like a potluck, not a restaurant. Church is not a buffet where you are served and offered an array of dishes where you can pick and choose whatever you want. At our church, you do not come in, sit at a table and expect others to wait on you to provide for your every whim and desire. No, the church is certainly not like a restaurant; at least not our church. However, one day the Church shall be served with a banquet, where the Lord will bless and provide for each person who has answered His invitation to the Wedding Feast of the Lamb (Revelation 19:7–9). But in the meantime, while we are still on this earth, the Church is to operate like a potluck.

The moral of the potluck analogy is this: If everyone brings something into the house, specifically a dish representing who they are, prepared with love and care, then there will always be more than enough to eat. What's more, you'll leave with more food and a greater variety of flavors than when you arrived. That, my friends, is how the church is supposed to be—like a potluck. This church-is-like-a-potluck analogy is right in line with Paul's instruction to the believers in Corinth found in 1 Corinthians 14:26, which essentially says that our contribution "is for the strengthening of the church." Potluck . . . it does a Body good.

I've found that most people want to make a difference and want to contribute to something bigger than themselves. They don't want to be spoon-fed and truly don't care to go to a smorgasbord where food is already prepared and all you do is grab an empty plate, eat all you can, then leave like a satisfied glutton! People would rather bring a dish, representing their gift or talent and watch others enjoy what they've prepared themselves. They want to return home full of what others have shared too. We, the church, provide the venue and set the table for just such a feast to flourish.

---

[1] Seasoned cubes of raw fish or octopus.

[2] Smoked, pulled-pork baked in an underground oven called an *imu*.

CHAPTER 14

MOMENTUM

The Wave You've Been Waiting For

"His master replied, 'Well done, good and faithful servant!
You have been faithful with a few things; I will put you in charge of many things.
Come and share your master's happiness!'"
Matthew 25:21

"Everyone to whom much was given, of him much will be required,
and from him to whom they entrusted much, they will demand the more."
Luke 12:48 ESV

Several years had gone by, and our steady plodding kept us focused on our goal: to reach as many people as possible, by any means possible, so that we might save some. As a result, the church began to grow slowly but surely. In retrospect, I am grateful for the steady growth the Lord allowed. The Lord knew exactly what He was doing, sending us the right people and the right amount. If we were given more than we had received in those first eight years, I'm not sure how well we would have stewarded all that was given to us.

Perhaps our capacity to shepherd, or our church's maturity level, had something to do with our growth rate. Maybe the Lord knew what I could handle mentally, spiritually, and emotionally, and needed us to wait for help to arrive to stabilize our extended, hard-working team. We certainly worked hard, but we also made sure the staff balanced family life along with ministry. Whatever the reason for the slow and steady growth, I wouldn't trade that season for anything in the world.

CHANGES

By 2007–2008, our weekend attendance grew to approximately 700, including children. As previously stated, we counted everybody. To this day, I still like to say, "At Hope Chapel West O'ahu, everybody counts!" The cafeteria in which we met held a maximum of 250 people, including the 30 people peering into windows from outside the sanctuary. From two Sunday services we grew to three at 7:30, 9, and 11 am. We prematurely started a 6 pm Saturday evening service that was sparsely attended for months. On occasion, the worship team outnumbered the congregation! Just when I was about to put a fork in it because it was D-O-N-E, attendance began to double, then triple within months. I just started

✺

On occasion, the worship team outnumbered the congregation!

✺

attending the University of Hawai'i Warrior football games on those slow Saturday nights. I was looking forward to bringing the Saturday evening services to an end. It was not meant to be. As a result, I didn't get to witness much of the Warrior's historic 12–0 season, but I did see the Bride blossom!

After a couple of years of having four services, we knew we could reach more but just didn't have the space, especially during our "optimum" Sunday services at 9 am and 11 am. It was killing me when the services reached 100-percent capacity only to see attendance drop to 75 to 85 percent a few weeks later. We kept hitting a ceiling and knew we needed more space. I could not accept that people were leaving because they could not find a seat in the house. We had to do something.[1]

New Sights and Sites

Faithfulness and fruitfulness—that's our story. We were faithful with the building we occupied on weekends and faithful in keeping those we reached. We believed that if we were faithful to do what the Lord called us to, He would also help us find creative solutions to steward those He sent. We knew the building limited our growth. Pastor Bill Hybels taught that for a church to reach its "full redemptive potential," it needs the maximum amount of seating at optimum service times. In Hawai'i, most people attend church on Sundays between the hours of 9 and 11 am. Armed with that knowledge, we set out to start a 10 am service at another location about five miles away. In our situation, necessity was the mother of innovation. This was an opportunity to pack three services into a two-hour time span. This plan involved a new site, new logistics, and hospitality teams, another worship team, and transportation to get me there and back.

We did exactly that. My typical Sunday now included preaching at 7:30 am, moving into the 9 am service with worship, announcements, my sermon, and an "Amen!" Then, out the back door and into a waiting car with a driver and a bottle of cold, pink Gatorade (because blue Gatorade would stain the clear orthodontics I was sporting at the time) to replenish my electrolytes from preaching. We'd make the five-mile trek north to our remote site, which was in a town of 70,000 people called Mililani, into a shopping mall where the University of Phoenix (U.O.P.) occupied an office space that held approximately 125 people. We had the place set up with a full stage, lights, sound equipment, welcome area, and classrooms for our Children's Church. It was a mini-version of our Waikele site. I usually arrived during the last worship song, or just before communion or announcements. At times I was late because I got excited and preached a little too long at the 9 am service, so someone would call from the school and notify the other service that I was running late. *No problemo*. They'd just add another worship song. After the sermon and the prayer, I'd jump back into a waiting car to head back to Waikele and preach my last sermon. That was five services every weekend; one on Saturday evenings and four on Sunday mornings. I would get home on Sunday afternoons completely exhausted.

This crazy routine would last for a few months until I realized I needed to share the load and switch to a team-teaching model. But I must say that the new service in a different location worked. God blessed our efforts and we began to grow at our U.O.P. location, so much so that we were regularly maxing out the room. We were faced with the same problem we were having at Waikele. We bumped up to overflow capacity, which caused attendance to drop to 80 percent. Argh! Yet, yay! What a great problem to have! Within the year, we had flirted with exceeding the 1,000-person growth mark that we had set for ourselves. Many more were surrendering their lives to Jesus every weekend, and the church was healthier than ever.

With me preaching three services and a staff pastor preaching at two, the team-teaching concept was beginning to work. The ministry was no longer revolving around me. People were stepping up to fill roles at U.O.P. and Waikele.

THE MIGHTY MO

Pearl Harbor is home to the historic U.S.S. Missouri battleship (the Mighty Mo) where Imperial Japan surrendered to the U.S., bringing World War II to a conclusion. Today, the Mighty Mo is a symbol of American service, sacrifice and pride, not only for America, but also for the state of Hawai'i. We treasure the Mighty Mo.

As the church grew I was looking for a different kind of "Mo." We prayed for it, worked at it, talked about it, looked toward the horizon for it, as if it were something coming from the east like the morning sun. And then it finally began happening at HCWO. It's called momentum.

Momentum is like this: Say your car just died, so you pull over to the side of the road, but you are just a hundred feet or less from the gas station. You wouldn't call a tow truck because that would seem foolish, so you push your car to get it to the gas station. However, your car is a lot heavier than you, so you look to see if anyone is willing to pull over and help you. Seeing that you are all by your lonesome, you straighten out your wheel, get in the space between the open door and the door jamb, and with your left hand on the door and right hand alternating between the jamb and the wheel, you push that car with all of the might you can

But as you keep applying muscle and determination to the object you are leaning into, it begins to roll.

muster. Leveraging your weight, you are nearly perpendicular to the pavement as every muscle in your thighs and calves strain to move the car a few inches. But as you keep applying muscle and determination to the object you are leaning into, it begins to roll.

Now, instead of being parallel to the asphalt, you've straightened up your torso; however, you are still bent over to keep the vehicle moving because it has picked up pace and, you notice that you're not working as hard as you first did. So, you continue adding pressure and when you see that you are on a roll, you straighten your back and find that the speed of the car is in sync and in rhythm with your stride, or, is it the other way around? Instead of pushing as hard as you once did, now most of your effort is on steering the vehicle in the right direction, avoiding the curb on the right side while looking ahead. You are near the gas station, and though you are sweating, your body is cooling because the car is closer to its destination and the great amount of physical exertion you once spent has paid off. Presently you are experiencing a much coveted, intangible commodity called *momentum.*

We had found momentum and were determined to keep it. The Mighty Mo was now our friend, and we did whatever we could to feed it. As momentum grew, a breakthrough was about to happen. We were rewarded by the Lord for our faithfulness. With momentum came courage and more growth. We had the courage to step out and do things we previously could not do.

---

[1] Miles McPherson, *Do Something: Make Your Life Count* (Grand Rapids, MI: Baker Books, 2009).

CHAPTER 15

THE FIGHT OF OUR LIVES

Increased Stress Leads to Increased Capacity

"God can do anything, you know—
far more than you could ever imagine or guess
or request in your wildest dreams!"
Ephesians 3:20 The Message

By 2007, we planted two churches in Australia and sponsored another church plant on O'ahu, a few miles away. We also helped to financially sponsor and inspire other young church planters. Though our primary focus was our own church, we also loved supporting and building God's Kingdom here in Hawai'i and beyond. At this point in time, we also knew the buildings we were renting for the weekend services would not take us to where we wanted to go. But before we released our old buildings, God wanted us to remove some old mindsets as well. For the first seven years of the church, I would drive past the Waikele Shopping Center where there were three buildings with a high turnover of renters. One building started off as a national chain computer and electronics store. They shut down when their business went belly up, and next thing we knew, it became a clothing store.

Another building was originally occupied by a grocery store. Later, it turned into a large furniture store. Every weekend, on my way to our small school cafeteria, I would drive by that furniture store, and yell out my passenger window, "In the name of Jesus, I claim those buildings for our church!" I had just a few seconds to calm myself down before entering the driveway to our school cafeteria church that the Lord had blessed us with. I did this every weekend, for seven years.

In August of 2007, I had just returned from vacation, the Hillsong Leadership Conference in Sydney, Australia, a personal planning retreat and a staff retreat. Needless to say, I was flying high and had heard from the Lord in a huge way. While on my planning retreat, I prayed and asked the Lord for a theme for the

<hr/>

While on this particular retreat, I heard two distinct words—*increase* and *enlarge.*

<hr/>

upcoming fiscal year. Receiving a specific word from the Lord about the theme was very important to me because I wanted to plan the rest of my preaching calendar and steer our staff-planning retreat around God's direction.

While on this particular retreat, I heard two distinct words—*increase* and *enlarge.* I wasn't sure if I had heard it correctly so I waited for confirmation. I began thinking, *Is this just me, or is it the Lord? Could this be my ambition rising up again?* It didn't make any sense. Our state economy was beginning to buckle, companies were downsizing and making cutbacks and real estate was still at an all-time high. In addition to that, I was struggling with what was "from the Lord" and what was my imagination. Confused and frustrated, I phoned a pastor friend who put me at ease. After his encouragement, I reasoned, *Hey, if I'm fasting and away from my family and denying myself by staying in this Spartan-like accommodation on the Kane'ohe Marine Base, why wouldn't the Lord speak to me?* I began perusing the Scriptures, looking for anything that would resonate in my heart. I happened upon two passages, and I could not believe my eyes:

". . . And (the Lord) said to me, 'I am going to make you fruitful and increase your numbers. I will make you a community of peoples, and I will give this land as an everlasting possession to your descendants after you.'"

Genesis 48:4

"Enlarge the place of your tent, stretch your tent curtains wide, do not hold back; lengthen your cords, strengthen your stakes. For you will spread out to the right and to the left; your descendants will dispossess nations and settle in their desolate cities."

Isaiah 54:2–3

I was filled with awe and fear. The awe was understandable—the fear was due to the magnitude of the words *increase* and *enlarge*. I would be too afraid to think them up myself! A large part of me felt I would have to back it up. However, it is the Lord who backs up His promises. They were His words for us at that specific time. Although I am fully aware that the words were spoken to the offspring of Jacob in the Genesis verses and to the Israelites in Isaiah, I believe the promises of God are for us today as well.

After all the retreats and our time in Sydney, we were ready to get to work. I was sermon-prepping during my first week back to work when I got a call from Randy one afternoon. "Mike," he said. "What are you doing? Are you sitting down? I have some bad news." I hate bad news. To me, bad news is like taking cough medicine as a kid, and the faster you give it to me, the easier it is to swallow. My blood pressure went up and I was on edge. "Just give it to me, Randy." He replied, "You're not going to believe this. The school just called to tell us they are raising our rent by 200 percent, and that was after I just dropped off the check for $5,000 to bless them!" I couldn't believe what I was hearing. I wanted to tell him to go and get that check back! I was floored, literally. Lisa, overhearing my end of the conversation, asked me, "What? What?"

I must admit that I "backslid" for about thirty seconds. When I regained my composure, I told Lisa what happened and said, "I thought the Lord said *increase* and *enlarge*. Not decrease and downsize!" I wasn't sure what we were going to do. I called Randy back and said, "That's it. We're outta there. We need to find another place, one much bigger. Let's start looking." So we began hunting throughout the island.

A Timely Word

This story brings to mind an event that took place a year before all of this transpired. We hosted a friend (who asked to remain anonymous) as a guest worship leader at our church for the weekend. The Lord was about to use him greatly in our church, we just didn't know it yet and neither did he.

He had ministered during all three services at Waikele and was about to lead his last song when he stopped and said through the microphone, "Pastor Mike, do you receive prophetic words here? Because I have a word for you that I believe is from the Lord." Wow. Talk about being put on the spot! For us quasi-Pentecostal types (just kidding), we aren't usually as spontaneous when it comes

❦

"The Lord says your dreams are too small."

❦

to prophecy. But because I loved his heart and was getting to know him better, combined with my respect for his father, I decided to give it a go. Otherwise, what else could I have said? "Uh, sorry. You have to meet with my head intercessors, let us pray about it to test it and see. . . ." No. At least not this time. "Sure," I replied. "Just give it to me."

This was one of those moments in life that are kept in a special internal photo album, that you bring out from time to time so you can say, "Ooh! This was the time when it . . . And, this was when He . . ." This was one of those times.

"The Lord says your dreams are too small."

I had mixed emotions as soon as he said it. On the one hand I thought, *"Humph! Well, I never! My dreams are too small? I have BIG dreams! It's obvious you don't know to whom it is you are prophesying! I'm Mike Kai!"* It was a split second before the tears started to roll down my face. *My dreams are too small? Are you serious? God has bigger plans for us?* The worship leader finished and prayed for me.

Here's one of my favorite verses:

> *"However, as it is written: 'No eye has seen, no ear has heard, no mind has conceived the things God has prepared for those who love him.'"*
>
> See 1 Corinthians 2:9

This verse, along with the parable of the talents, kept running around in my mind. This promise from God to all believers has been a foundational Scripture for our life and church. Here's my translation: "If you let Him, God will blow your mind, simply because He loves you." In the midst of the bad news about the school, the Lord was carefully placing thorns in our nest so that we would learn to get out of the nest and soar, once again.

"IT'S YOURS, BRO"

A while back I had inquired about the leasing for one of the buildings in the Waikele Shopping Center, the one I had yelled at and claimed as ours. The furniture store folded a year prior and the property now stood vacant, so I thought we might as well give it a try. We created a DVD that had me standing in front of the building talking to *the powers that be* with the hopes that they would consider leasing their 37,000 square-foot building to our church. Of course, at the time, there was no way we could even entertain the thought of leasing a building that size because retail space in Hawai'i is very expensive. But I figured, *no guts, no glory, right?* It was like I was a freshman asking the prom queen for a dance when her boyfriend (who happened to be the prom king) stood right next to her. (Yes, I actually did just that in high school. Not too smart.)

Proverbs mentions that bribes or gifts can open doors. We FedEx-ed the DVD and a gift basket filled with the best Hawaiian treats to the leasing company. We meant it as a gift; a gesture of Hawaiian hospitality, if you will. A very long month went by and I had no reply. I figured it was a good time to give them a call.

Interestingly, my good friend Roger Archer from Puyallup Foursquare Church in the state of Washington was with me one weekend, and I drove him by the old furniture building. Roger pastors one of the great churches of the Pacific Northwest and one of the best churches in our denomination. He is one of our top leaders. When we arrived at the building, he got out of the car, laid his hands on the building, and began praying for it with authority! I stood there, nodding

I was also on the lookout for security guards wondering what two grown men were doing with their hands on the walls.

my approval to his prayer. I was also on the lookout for security guards wondering what two grown men were doing with their hands on the walls. We looked like two guys being held up at gunpoint, with no gunman! When he was done, he walked away, looked over his shoulder, and said, "It's yours, Bro. Done."

That's Roger. In fact, he was one of the key people who encouraged me during every step of the process. When I got down on myself, I'd call Roger and he'd yell at me saying, "What's wrong with you, boy? Pull up your pants and have big faith! God is going to give that to you. I saw it, I believe it, end of discussion." If it weren't for Ralph Moore and Roger Archer, I would have been an emotional basket case during that season. That's the truth. I hope to one day play the same role in other people's lives when they come to major crossroads of their faith: "What's wrong with you, boy?" I love it!

I received no answer from the leasing company and kept calling. I left voice messages and sent e-mails, but to no avail. The company that owned the shopping center was like Fort Knox! It was nearly impossible to get through to them. But one day I received a call from the property manager of the shopping center. "Hi, I'm just calling to inform you that we have received your DVD and gift, but we aren't interested in renting out the space to a church at the moment. We wish you luck in your search for a new home." I quickly replied, "Just a minute, please. Do you have anyone else in mind? Is there another store coming in?" She then began to tell me that they were hoping for a big-box retail store. I said, "Nah, that won't work. That corner of the shopping center is terrible." She said, "Can you afford it?" Taken somewhat aback from the touché in the conversation, I said, "Of course, we can. With God all things are possible." She then politely ended the conversation and I told her I would be calling in a few months to see if the place was still available. After the call my heart sank. For a few months, I

I quit yelling at the building as I drove by. I would ignore it, either pretending it wasn't there or that we didn't need it.

quit yelling at the building as I drove by. I would ignore it, either pretending it wasn't there or that we didn't need it. I was leery of getting my hopes up. Defeating thoughts entered my mind: *Maybe we're out of our league? Who did we think we were, trying for a building like that? Set your sights lower. Find something smaller.* But the problem was that the building was still there and wasn't moving.

Even though my hopes for a bigger building like the one at the shopping center were gone, the reality still remained. We needed more space. So we began a search while "dumbing down" our vision. Well, actually I began to dumb it down. I began aiming lower for something more "realistic," something much closer to our price range. With the increased cost of renting the current school facility, our combined leases totaled somewhere around $10,000 a month. I couldn't see us spending that kind of money on a school and an office space. We looked at a building across the street from our office in an industrial district, but they promised it to a gymnastics business. We looked at a warehouse next door, but every attempt seemed to fail. We kept our eyes open for anything that could seat at least 500 people per service. But in Hawai'i, not a lot of real estate options exist for what we were looking for, and if we were to purchase land, we were looking at spending a minimum of ten million dollars to build. We didn't have that kind of money.

150

What a Trip!

I had a trip scheduled to Indonesia for a conference of Asian churches and missionaries in the city of Medan. In the midst of our search, I headed to Indonesia because I had already paid for the trip and I have a passion for church-planters and missionaries. That led me to start a non-profit organization alongside of HCWO called Send Hope International.

After a series of long flights, I arrived at the conference with delegates from all over the South Pacific and Southeast Asia. I was having a great time, when I heard the news of the stock market crash in October 2008, which we now refer to as the Global Financial Crisis. With an eighteen-hour time difference and spotty Internet connection at best, I was unable to move my retirement investment selections from one account to another in order to stop the bleeding. Like many Americans, I lost up to 40 percent of my retirement savings within three days. But what worried me more were the finances of the church. We had monies tied up in certificates of deposit that were relatively safe. While in Indonesia the Lord spoke to me and said, "I'll place the church in Goshen where you will be safe and multiply" (see Genesis 45:10). *Goshen*, I thought. Isn't that the place where Joseph's family and Jacob's offspring lived in Genesis? And, didn't they enjoy safe pasture and multiply like rabbits while there? I was at peace even though I was worried, if that makes any sense. I kept calling the office to make sure we were okay, but there was really nothing I could do about it from Indonesia. I felt helpless, but the Lord was truly in control. Goshen sounded good to me.

Back Home

After arriving home from my trip to Asia, I picked up the paper one morning to learn that a new clothing store was coming to the Waikele Shopping Center. They would renovate and lease the 25,000-square-foot building next to the former furniture store. After two months, I picked up the local paper again, and read that the clothing store was closing its stores nationwide due to bankruptcy. That got me excited.

So I drove down to the store to do some investigating. When I arrived, I walked in and began looking at clothing until I found an employee. After the obligatory, "Hi, finding everything alright?" from the salesgirl, I said in a hushed, apologetic tone, "I heard you guys are filing for bankruptcy. I'm so sorry to hear that." She replied, "Oh, no. Our store will remain open." To which I countered,

So, as a guilt offering, I did what I felt was the only right thing to do— I bought myself a shirt.

"Oh, good! That's good to hear. Alright, bye." But inside I was saying, "Argh!" But after leaving the girl I started to feel bad over such a self-serving move. So, as a guilt offering, I did what I felt was the only right thing to do—I bought myself a shirt.

A little disappointed, I walked over to my car and was about to open the car door when I noticed something: an open door. It was no ordinary door. It was the door to the furniture store, where all of my hopes and dreams could be furnished. You have to understand that up to this point, I had never seen any of their doors open. I'd see lights from the freeway on whenever I'd drive by, but never an open door. Here was our chance. And whenever you see an open door, you walk through it.

"Hi! Mind if I take a look inside?" I asked the man who was fixing the open door. "No, I don't work here." I told him it didn't matter; I wouldn't tell anyone if he let me in. He explained that the boss would be back and then I could look inside. "Oh, come on," I said. "I'll just run right in and run right out. In fact, you can watch me the entire time. Really, do I look like someone who would steal something?" The man was not to be convinced. "Okay, how about if I just stepped right here, ten feet away from you, and just had a quick look." Persistence pays off. While I stood near the worker, I scanned the dark place and prayed what I like to call machine-gun tongues, meaning, I said a prayer in the Spirit, from left to right, like I was spraying bullets from a machine gun:

"Parattatattattattatt . . . tat." Satisfied, I turned around and headed out. As I left, the doorkeeper shouted, "Hey, the boss will be back from lunch in an hour!" I thanked him and got in my car. I couldn't be back in an hour. I had an appointment. *Maybe it's not meant to be*, I thought briefly. But God had other plans. Better plans.

As it turned out, the "Boss" pulled up in his white Chevy truck right as I got to my car. I approached him and said, "Hi! I'm Mike Kai. Is this place for rent?" He said, "Yes it is. The economy is so bad right now that we have to lease this place out as soon as we can." What'd I tell ya? I'm a man of God with great faith!

We began negotiations but at one point I thought it was over. One of the big-box retail stores in the shopping complex had a clause inserted into their contract that stated no "House of Worship" would be allowed to become a tenant. I was flabbergasted. This, I reasoned, had to be demonic in origin. I'm not sure if the clause had to do with parking, or with just being anti-religion (which

❧

Slowly, my faith level was chipped away to the point of near depression. I was at my lowest point.

❧

wouldn't surprise me these days), but whatever the reason, it was holding up our destiny. Days and weeks passed by and we could not get through. No e-mails or phone calls were returned. Slowly, my faith level was chipped away to the point of near depression. I was at my lowest point.

SPEAK TO ME

I woke up one morning, still discouraged, and got ready to take Bekah to school. While walking out the door, I repeated to Lisa, "We're going to lose it, Babe. We're not going to get it." My wife is one feisty, Chinese woman. She's gorgeous, too. She said, "Stop it, Mike. Listen to yourself. Do you hear what you're saying?" I had a hard time believing it. After dropping Bekah off at the school, I pulled over to a gas station to call our realtor. "I'll fly up to their headquarters in Ohio if that's what it takes. This is ridiculous. Maybe I can bring a Hawaiian gift basket. Gee, that always seems to work." He said to just be patient. Yeah, right. He was just as dumbfounded as I was, but in retrospect he would prove to be right.

As was my normal routine, I got to the gym and made a weak attempt at a workout. I put on my earphones and listened to Tommy Walker's "Speak To Me."[1] Bad move. I sat on the bench, covered my head with my workout towel and began crying because of the words to the song. I mean, who cries in a gym? I couldn't control myself. I was embarrassed and got myself out of there, red-

I sat on the bench, covered my head with my workout towel and began crying. I mean, who cries in a gym?

eyed, runny nose and all. I went home because Lisa and I needed to be at a luncheon at eleven. So after a few hours of working on my sermon, we got in the car and headed out.

The song "Speak to Me" ministered to me so much that as I drove I played the song again. Lisa put her hand on my arm and said to her dejected Man of God-Full of Faith, "It's okay, Honey. It'll be alright." The tears reappeared. As we drove the song came on and I said, "Babe, listen to this. The Lord really blessed me at the gym with this." I guess I'm a glutton for punishment because I had to put my sunglasses on because I started crying more and I couldn't stop! But my combination of self-pity and worship came to a halt as I was irritated by the ring on my phone. It was our realtor.

"Hey, Big Guy. What are you doing?" he said.

"I'm in the car with Lisa. Why? What's up?" I replied in a not-so-friendly tone.

"Where you going?"

"To lunch. Why?" How soon I forgot he was doing this for free.

"Can you talk?"

He sounded more chipper than I was, so I was curious, and irritated. "Yes, I can talk. I'm talking with you now, right? Go ahead." Lisa rolled her eyes at me.

"Ok. We got the place! The big-box retailer guys signed a document saying they have waived the clause to the 'No House of Worship' thingy!"

The tears reappeared and I had to pull over to the side of the road because I couldn't drive. Besides, I needed to thank the Lord in prayer and do it with the realtor on the phone.

God is so good and so faithful.

> *"His master replied, 'Well done, good and faithful servant! You have been faithful with a few things; I will put you in charge of many things. Come and share your master's happiness!'"*
>
> Matthew 25:21

> *"However, as it is written: 'No eye has seen, no ear has heard, no mind has conceived the things God has prepared for those who love him.'"*
>
> See 1 Corinthians 2:9

---

[1] Tommy Walker, "Speak to Me," *I Have a Hope*, 2008.

CHAPTER 16

THE BEST IS YET TO COME

Always Content But Never Complacent

"Your beginnings will seem humble, so prosperous will your future be."

Job 8:7

"And though you started with little, you will end with much."

Job 8:7 NLT

W e often hear people say, "God won't give you more than you can handle." Although it's not directly from Scripture, the statement is usually offered by someone genuinely concerned for our welfare when we're experiencing personal pain. It's like a topical ointment used to bring temporary relief and perspective. To some extent, within this particular context, I believe it to be true. Why? Because the Lord does know just how much we can endure.

On the other hand, I think there is a certain amount of truth in saying that God *will give you more than you can handle* because He wants to work greatly in your life. It is at these moments in your development that He wants you to rely on Him for total victory. Almost every major character in

156

the Bible faced things that were way more than they could handle on their own.

There is one more way we can apply the same saying in the light of the parable of the talents. What is also true is that God will *not* give us more than we can handle if we can't steward well what He would like to give us. Why? He doesn't want what He gives us to go to waste. The same applies in the kitchen. If I have a quart container but a gallon of milk, it would be wasteful and foolish of me to pour the entire gallon of milk into a container that cannot hold or *steward* what I would like to pour into it. I'll need a vessel or container that is equal to, or larger than, the quart container.

Like the three servants in the parable of the talents, each one had a different *capacity* to steward what they were given. The servants with one talent and two talents were not given five talents because they didn't have the capacity to stew-

✒

God will *not* give us more than we can handle if we can't steward well what he would like to give us.

✒

ard well what they might have been given. They got what they got. The master gives according to an individual servant's capacity for good stewardship.

Our old building did not have the capacity to handle the 5,000 or more people that today call HCWO their home church. There wasn't enough square footage, seating capacity, parking, or room to grow. It was too small. We did everything we could: five services every weekend in two locations to get to 1,000. Unless 400 people in the church received a revelation from God to attend the 7:30 am service to make room at the 9 and 11 am services, this was as far as we could go. We had been faithful stewards, and now, the reward had arrived!

Looking back on the history of our church, there were two critical years within the first eight in which the Lord took us to a *ho' nutha level.*[1] During that period we grew in leadership and matured as a church. We kept the fires of evangelizing the lost white-hot and did our best to steward both those who were new believers or those churched for a while.

We added a new axiom to our vocabulary that we would emphasize every six months or so—upgrade. We looked around the cafeteria (our converted sanctuary) and asked ourselves, "Where can we upgrade? What needs upgrading?" It could've been technology or the stage presentation. It could've been our leadership training or discipleship, our attitudes or our outlook, our generosity or compassion. Everything. Then we'd prioritize and address it from that point. This was and still is considered faithfulness.

A retrospective view is always so much clearer from a good distance away. One thing that is vivid now was our realization that we were indeed ready to receive the gift of our current location. The staff would all agree that we were already playing at a *ho' nutha level* in the cafeteria at the school. We never for a moment thought that we were too good for the building we were in. We were so thankful to be there. We were great stewards of the school and appreciative

What seemed difficult and painful in the past, has become the new normal and even something that we have built upon.

to the Lord for it. It was when we had maxed out our capacity to receive more people, combined with an expansion of our leadership and heart for the Lord's people, that we were given more than we imagined. The two talents had then become four talents. And to Him be the Glory.

MORE THAN WE COULD HANDLE

God does sometimes give us more than we can handle. Throughout the process of pastoring the church, there were times we encountered situations that seemed like more than we could handle. In those times, He was there to make up for our deficit. To go for a building like the one we are now leasing took huge faith on our part. As you read in the previous chapter, the process was almost more than I could stand. As I look back on the season, our faith and ability to endure more has increased greatly. What seemed difficult and painful in the past, has become the new normal and even something that we have built upon. We can now stand higher and see farther because the trials in the past, which seemed so daunting at the time, have increased our ability (capacity) to handle even more.

So why would the Lord give us more than we can handle? I believe it's two-fold. One, it increases our ability to endure more in the future. If you can over-come this trial, it only increases your strength for more in the future. Secondly, it's because the struggle and pain you may be currently going through draws you nearer to Him. God delights to be near His children. Brokenness and humility, dependency and desperation, all cause us to rely more on Him and His power. So it's for the purpose of increased capacity and deeper dependency. That's what hap-pened to our church and that's what happened to me. As a result, we have a story to tell of the faithfulness of God and a building we call home. "With man this is impossible, but with God all things are possible" (Matthew 19:26).

INSPIRATION IS A WISE INVESTMENT

I love inspiring people to answer the call of God on their lives. I get great satis-faction when a sermon I've preached, a lesson I've taught, or the coffee time I've shared with a young leader has inspired them to do something with their life for Jesus. We need more pastors and business people achieving their full potential. We need to exhort young people to see beyond their cynical views of the future and to push on regardless of economic forecasts or current international affairs. We need to challenge broken and disheartened people to push through their cir-cumstances and see that *God is for them* and has an awesome plan for their lives. But this cannot happen until someone gets inspired.

You see, if you or I get inspired by God through a book, a conference, a sermon, or an insight from the Lord, then it will translate into action. Action brings about change and change involves people. It should lift people. Inspiration is that first domino that gets nudged in the right direction creating a domino effect. Inspiration sets off a chain of events that inevitably affects every other domino in its path.

When I get inspired, look out. Somebody is going to get pushed, nudged, and possibly kicked in the right direction. *Nothing really happens until someone gets inspired.* Don't ever underestimate the power of inspiration. If something or someone is God-inspired then that life becomes a God-inspired sacrifice to the Lord. It begins with inspiration. And, sometimes you have to "pay" to be inspired.

Lisa, Ben Houston from Hillsong Church, author and speaker John Bevere, and I were enjoying lunch after one of our conferences when Lisa said, "John, I'd love to have your wife, Lisa, speak at our first women's conference next year!" John then asked her if she had ever heard Lisa speak before. On a side note, I have, and let me say, Lisa Bevere is possibly one of the most gifted and powerful speakers I have ever heard, period. My Lisa said that she had not, and John suggested one of the best things that could have ever happened to us. He said, "Then, Lisa, you have to go to the Colour Women's Conference hosted by Ben's mom, pastor Bobbie Houston of Hillsong. In fact, I truly believe you have to be there." There was one problem. We had planned a lifelong dream trip of mine to Argentina for a week, and this would be one of the first times Lisa and I would be leaving our two younger daughters at home. This wasn't easy for Lisa, but she knew it would be good for us. Our vacation was planned a week before the Colour Conference in Sydney, Australia.

My wife hemmed and hawed for about a minute. I jumped in and told her I had the girls, she could get on the plane the day we got home from Buenos Aires and head out for Sydney all by herself. Actually, I really wanted her to go because I felt it could be an incredible time for her to be alone with the Lord. We had the means to do so, so she should go, I thought. Ben added, "I can get you in. It's sold out but I'll make some arrangements and I'm sure you'll love it." Surrounded by three men who were emphatically encouraging her to go, she gave in and said yes. I'm so glad she did.

Lisa rarely called me when she was at Colour, knowing that the girls were doing fine with me. I prayed for her and missed her tremendously but I somehow knew the Lord was doing great things with her there.

When she returned, she didn't talk much about it until about the third day. I sensed she needed to process her thoughts and prayers before we could have a good conversation. Over a cup of tea, she finally said, "I've been afraid to tell you what the Lord said to me when I was at Colour, because I know that once I say it, I'll be held accountable and it will have to happen." I braced myself. "The Lord told me I need to step up and take a larger role in the church," Lisa continued. "He said I needed to speak to you about starting a women's church service, once a month or so, to encourage the women. And, I need to speak more." I had no problem with the first two ideas, but I was a little apprehensive about the third point. But I shouldn't have been. Two years prior to this defining moment for Lisa (for all of us, actually), the Lord spoke to me at my first Hillsong conference when I was alone and impressed upon me, "Platform your wife. I want Lisa to have a voice." I told her what the Lord said and she was hesitant. After a few more attempts and the resulting pushback, I backed off. But this time, she heard directly from the Lord and we were on the same page.

We didn't come from a model of church where the pastor's wife spoke or where she was the women's pastor. Lisa, like me, is an ordained minister in our denomination, and as I previously stated, a woman founded our denomination. The issue of women in leadership and teaching in the church was not an issue for us like it might be elsewhere. The problem was not the model, but the vessel. Lisa

In this case, the inspiration we paid for, paid off.

wasn't ready. But in order for Lisa to be ready, the Lord had to ready and prepare me. Could I handle it? Could I allow room for Lisa and Arise (the eventual name of her ministry, conference, and monthly service)? Was I secure enough in my role to encourage her to accept her new role? The answer was a definite yes.

Since Lisa has answered the Lord's personal call on her life to Arise, women across Hawai'i have done the same. By the hundreds they've attended and have been equipped, inspired, and empowered to become all God has called them to be. It has actually been one of the most amazing things I have witnessed in the past three years of our church. And I attribute much of it to a housewife (a very noble occupation, I might add) who answered a call to lead other housewives and business women to Arise, to become all God intends them to be. And, all because she got inspired. In this case, the inspiration we paid for, paid off.

I had no idea the effect the Hillsong Colour Conference would have on Lisa. If you know my wife, you'll notice that she's not the frilly type. Women's

161

conferences were not her thing. However, that all changed when John and Ben convinced her that she needed to attend and see what it was about. After much contemplation, she decided that she would see for herself.

We are so glad that she did! As a result, she was inspired to host our own women's conference. She named it *Arise* because that is exactly what happened to her. The Lord called her to *arise* to a place of leadership she had never risen to previously. Through *Arise*, many other women like her in our church and the state are fulfilling the P4P Value. They are awakening and arising to their God-given calling and potential and it is affecting our church in an incredible way! I believe we have a much healthier "house" because of her role as the mother-of-the-house.

I personally get inspired by watching families stay together and prevail through tough times. The road may be bumpy for a season or two, but I love to see them on the other side of the struggle, standing stronger and taller having gone through the fire of affliction. That really inspires me.

My wife and daughters have the ability to inspire me. And I want to inspire them. Not discourage them. When Lisa brags about me in front of other people, I feel so good! In my position (and some of you experience the same thing), I get appreciation from people all the time. I am grateful for it. I don't live for it, but it does provide "fuel in my tank" that can last for weeks! But when Lisa or my girls display their appreciation or admiration, man, look out! I can do anything: leap over a wall, climb the tallest mountain, swim the widest sea—anything! That inspires me. There's even a certain look that Lisa gives me that really inspires me. But I digress.

Who or what inspires you today? If it's a church or ministry, do what you can to go see it. Nothing really significant happens unless you're inspired. We have spent a lot of money sending our staff to places to get equipped and inspired, which has in turn impacted our church. Sometimes it takes money for that to happen but it can be the best investment with great returns if you're willing to do it.

Inspiration can come from just a walk alone on the beach or in the mountains. Creativity often flows when we are in the midst of the Creator's creativity. I treasure the walks alone or with Lisa on the beach. Whether alone or together, walking hand-in-hand on the sand with our feet in the water, God is with us, and a divine chemistry happens that brings inspiration, which in turn becomes action to invent something, write a sermon, or sing a song. On the downside, sometimes Lisa gets inspired on these walks and I find myself raking the leaves or painting the bathroom because of it. That's not the kind of inspiration I'm looking for.

Who are you inspiring? It doesn't have to be another church or ministry. It can be the single mother in row six, seat two. It could be a "Timothy" whom you have decided to invite to your home to help you change the oil in your car. I appreciate that Pastor Ralph taught me how to change the oil in my old Volvo.

><Se

Who are you inspiring? It doesn't have to be another church or ministry. It can be the single mother in row six, seat two.

><Se

While he was instructing me I didn't know it, but he was also discipling me in the process. Go get inspired by someone and inspire someone else in return. Kick off a chain reaction to something that has lasting impact.

INFLUENCE

A visiting pastor who is older than I am came to our church after we had occupied the new building for a year. Amazed at what he saw, he said, "You know, this is not just for you." Not expecting the statement, my knee-jerk answer was a confident, "I know." Too busy to respond further since the exchange was between services, I walked away slightly perplexed. It was a few months later before I fully understood the "Yoda-like" statement. This building, our story, was not to be kept. It was to be shared. The gifts, talents, and abilities the Lord gave us were not to be hoarded, hidden, dumbed-down, or worst of all, buried. They were to be fuel to inspire others.

Our worst enemies can be our own insecurities and perception of others. I hesitated to launch our now very successful Equip and Inspire conferences because I was worried what others would think. I'm so glad I overcame that. If I let others' opinions about myself or the church drive my decisions, I don't believe we would be where we are today.

Additionally, I don't think the Lord would have been delighted in my fear of man's opinions. The fear of man replaces Him as my Source. I should fear the Lord and His opinions more than what others have to say. Regardless of how others might feel about us, we still honor everyone. Also, if I let my little Gideon-like I-am-nobody mentality hold me back, it would hold our church back even more. Trust me when I say there's a constant tension between humble-gutsy Christ-like servanthood and self-glorification. Groveling on the ground and repeating, "I am a nobody, our church is nothing" isn't honoring to the Lord because it diminishes His glory and cost on the Cross. Yes, we are truly, without Christ, nobodies. And without Him in my life as my Savior, I shudder to think where I would be. But He *is* with us with limitless power and victory in His hands!

We strive to walk both in true humility and in this Old Testament promise, "The Lord will make you the head and not the tail; you shall be above only and not be beneath" (Deuteronomy 28:13 NKJV). That's the sweet spot we are looking for. We realize all that we've been given and it compels us to use what we have for the glory of God. Now we have some influence outside our own church. We weren't looking for it, but God entrusts us with it.

STEWARDS FOR INFLUENCE

It was surprising to us, but pastors were calling for advice even before the building and the growth. We decided to take the influence God had given us and four years ago started a nonprofit called Send Hope International to support church-planters and missionaries. My original idea was to alleviate the pressure on our church missions budget for our international travels because the churches we planted or discipled couldn't afford to pay for us to get there. So instead of HCWO paying for the whole thing, we set up a separate entity that could receive funds to send us to equip and inspire other pastors and leaders.

The biggest way of stewarding the influence we've been given is through our Equip and Inspire (E&I) Resources and Conferences. The E&I Leadership

Conference has become a staple in Hawai'i for church leaders. Our inaugural E&I Arise Women's Conference with Lisa Kai and Lisa Bevere packed the sanctuary with over 900 women in attendance! Our first ever Leadership Praxis was a crucial time of inspiration and unity for pastors from Hawai'i and abroad. Besides great local pastors, we've hosted such notable pastors as John Bevere, Brian Houston, Miles McPherson, Paul DeJong, Benny Perez, and Ben Houston.

If influence is given, it must be stewarded. If it is abused, misused, or mishandled it will be taken away. For an eye-opening example of this, read the story of Gehazi, the servant of Elisha in 2 Kings 5. If influence is not steadily reinvested time after time, the privilege could be passed on to another. I also understand that

If influence is given, it must be stewarded.

our role as influencers is not guaranteed till Kingdom come—there are times in God's sovereignty where He will shift anointing and influence somewhere else. That's His prerogative to do so.

There may one day be a season to pass it on; leadership, influence, whatever, because you can't keep it all to yourself and it will eventually need to be released. I think it's better for me and you if we give it freely when the time comes, not holding longer than necessary when it's clear the time has come to let it go. But the timing has to be right. You can't release prematurely and you can't hold on to it too long.

At this moment, I say to myself, *Hold it loosely, Mike. Hold it loosely. Don't let it be taken away from you or ripped from your hands. Don't treat it with contempt and become complacent because there are others just as hungry and capable. Don't drop it on the ground from carelessness and certainly don't throw it to the ground out of frustration or exhaustion. Steward it well, Mike. Contend for the honor of handing it to someone one day and whispering into his ear, "If you mess it up, I will hurt you, boy!"* Nah! Just kidding. Kick him on the backside to give him a start and begin yelling, "Run! Run like the wind, son! Don't look back;

keep your eyes straight ahead. Run with passion and abandon! But remember to hold it loosely!" Then watch quietly as he puts distance between himself and you, and smile.

REACH FOR YOUR REDEMPTIVE POTENTIAL

We have been blessed beyond our wildest expectations to pastor so many wonderful people. We love them so much. We have the most hardworking, dedicated and genuinely kind staff I've ever seen. But have we arrived? Not by any means! Are you kidding me? We're still young. There are leaders to raise, churches to plant, and souls to be saved. We have yet to reach our full redemptive potential.[2]

Every human being on this earth has potential to be all they were created for, but for one reason or another, either fail to attain it or, they become all that the Lord created them to be. *Potential* is always there. Always. In fact, Lisa married me based on potential; not necessarily what I was, but what I *could* be (and trust

What numerical value could we assign to the first church Jesus ever started over two millennia ago in the Upper Room in Jerusalem?

me, every now and then I tease her with, "How do you like me now?"). So if a person has potential, then so does the church. Add all the people, with untold amounts of potential, into a body of people called the Church and what you've got is a Church teeming with potential!

A church's full *redemptive potential could be realized* if, during the lifespan of that church, they were to reach everyone they were supposed to reach. And if that church encouraged the next generation and passed on the mantle of leadership to them, what could that look like? Would it look like ten thousand souls in the life of that church? Fifty thousand? A million?

Consider this: What numerical value could we assign to the first church Jesus ever started over two millennia ago in the Upper Room in Jerusalem? Well, they began with 120. Today, it's in the *untold* billions!

So what's your potential? What's the redemptive potential of your church? What can you do with the life you've been given, whether it's one, two or five talents? Because it doesn't matter what you've been given. What matters is what you do with what you've got. Faithfulness. Stewardship. Multiplication. That's the pound for pound principle.

---

[1] I learned this term at my first Hillsong Conference in 2006 when Ed Young from Dallas, Texas, kept repeating the phrase. It's stuck with me ever since.

[2] Bill Hybels, *The DNA of Effective Leadership*, http://www.christiantoday.com/article/bill.hybels.the.dna.of.effective.leadership/18203.htm.

EPILOGUE

After an epic weekend of seven Easter services, HCWO welcomed several thousands of people through its doors while leading 251 souls to a decision to make Jesus their Lord and Savior. Later that Sunday evening, as I stood over the sink washing the last of the day's dishes, my then fourteen-year-old Rebekah said to me, "Dad, you were really good today." I paused before replying, "Babe, I don't know how I could not have done well. I honestly do not know of any pastor who gets more prayer coverage, intercessors praying during every service, and incredible support than your mother and I receive. Although I'm always nervous before a sermon, I'm not surprised what Jesus did." She understood exactly what I was talking about. To God be the glory.

For each and every one of us, there is so much more vision to receive and so many more people to reach. After more than ten years of consistent hard work, our church prays that this is only the beginning. We have yet to reach our full redemptive potential. But we will contend until the end. At this writing, we have planted another church overseas, this time in Manila. Our young pastors, Noland and Jay Galido, are embarking on their very own journey to see what God can do for a city they've fallen in love with and a people they are reaching for Jesus. We are currently negotiating to purchase our building, or something greater, having begun what we call our Heart for the House initiative, our capital campaign to raise the resources necessary to give us options for our ever-increasing congregation. We have run out of space at our 37,000-square-foot location at the Waikele Shopping Center and are nearly maxed out with six weekend celebration services. We are in search of another location as I write to leverage everything the Lord has given us. That's the pound for pound principle in action—doing the best with what God has given us.

No matter what your current circumstance in life is, I hope this book has given you the inspiration to look at everything you have and invest it back into His Kingdom. Use the talents and gifts he has given you to be the best in your "weight class." Start right where you are. Do the very best with what He has given you and you will achieve and become the best version of you in this season.

You may encounter discouragement from time to time, but remember Proverbs 24:15–16: "No matter how many times you trip them up, God-loyal people don't stay down long; soon they're up on their feet" (The Message). Get yourself a good corner person or two, pick yourself up, get back in that ring, and fight! That giant in the ring is smaller than you think it is. Keep punching away at your obstacle. Remain flexible. And, remember this—all the defeats, trials, and frustrations you have endured, all of it, has been the Lord's way of increasing your capacity and ability to handle exactly what's in front of you. And lastly, don't forget, *you were born for this.*

Your story and our story continues...

Our Heart

For over a decade, Mike Kai has had a vision to develop healthy, thriving churches both locally and globally. This led him to create Send Hope International, a non-profit organization whose aim is to resource church planters and missionaries to reach the End-Times Harvest in Hawaii, the Pacific Rim, and beyond.

Send Hope International's scope of influence reaches as far east as Thailand and as south as Australia, where Mike teaches church health and multiplication strategies.

In addition to Mike's investment and training of leaders abroad, he and his wife, Lisa, host three impacting conferences in beautiful Hawaii: the Equip & Inspire Conference for pastors and leaders in the church, the Arise Women's Conference, and the Leadership Praxis - a conference designed specifically for the senior pastor and his executive team. Through these opportunities, thousands of leaders have been influenced and inspired to maximize their God-given potential.

www.mikekai.tv

EQUIP&INSPIRE

hope chapel
west oahu